Binge Eating

The Ultimate Guide to Finally Ending Emotional Eating, Bingeing, Overeating, and Food Addiction, Including Tips on Eating Disorder Recovery, and an Introduction to Mindful Eating

© Copyright 2020

This document is geared towards providing exact and reliable information in regard to the topic and issue covered. The publication is sold with the idea that the publisher is not required to render accounting, officially permitted, or otherwise, qualified services. If advice is necessary, legal or professional, a practiced individual in the profession should be ordered.

From a Declaration of Principles which was accepted and approved equally by a Committee of the American Bar Association and a Committee of Publishers and Associations.

In no way is it legal to reproduce, duplicate, or transmit any part of this document in either electronic means or in printed format. Recording of this publication is strictly prohibited and any storage of this document is not allowed unless with written permission from the publisher. All rights reserved.

The information provided herein is stated to be truthful and consistent, in that any liability, in terms of inattention or otherwise, by any usage or abuse of any policies, processes, or directions contained within is the solitary and utter responsibility of the recipient reader. Under no circumstances will any legal responsibility or blame be held against the publisher for any reparation, damages, or monetary loss due to the information herein, either directly or indirectly.

Respective authors own all copyrights not held by the publisher.

The information herein is offered for informational purposes solely, and is universal as so. The presentation of the information is without contract or any type of guarantee assurance.

The trademarks that are used are without any consent, and the publication of the trademark is without permission or backing by the trademark owner. All trademarks and brands within this book are for clarifying purposes only and are owned by the owners themselves, not affiliated with this document.

Contents

INTRODUCTION	1
CHAPTER ONE: INTRODUCTION TO BINGE EATING	4
Characteristics of Binge Eating	7
How the Binge Happens	9
Binge Eating Triggers	11
The End of a Binge	12
Eating Disorders and Eating Problems	13
CHAPTER TWO: MEET THE NINE MYTHS	17
Popular Binge Eating Myths	17
A Shift in Perspective	21
Two Prongs of the Problem	23
CHAPTER THREE: BED AND BODY WEIGHT	26
Key Facts About Body Weight	26
Quick Facts About Weight Loss and Dieting	27
Body Weight and Binge Eating	31
CHAPTER FOUR: BINGE EATING AND SCIENCE	33
The Biology of the Binge	33

- ON LEPTIN AND GHRELIN 34
- BINGING AND BRAIN FUNCTIONS 37
- PSYCHOLOGICAL FACTORS THAT SUSTAIN BED 38

CHAPTER FIVE: PHYSICAL EFFECTS OF BED 44
- EFFECTS OF FOOD DEPRIVATION AND UNHEALTHY WEIGHT LOSS 44

CHAPTER SIX: LOVING YOURSELF 54
- BODY IMAGE PROBLEMS 54
- BECOME ACQUAINTED WITH YOUR BODY 57
- TAKING CARE OF YOUR BODY 58
- EXTRA HELPFUL TIPS 58
- 10 CELEBRITIES AND EATING DISORDERS 60

CHAPTER SEVEN: INTUITIVE EATING 66
- TEN PRINCIPLES OF INTUITIVE EATING 67
- 6 INTUITIVE EATING MYTHS 70

CHAPTER EIGHT: MINDFULNESS 75
- AN UNDERSTANDING OF MINDFULNESS 76
- THE TENETS OF MINDFULNESS 77
- INSIGHT INTO MINDFUL MEDITATION 78
- HOW MINDFULNESS CAN HELP YOU 79

CHAPTER NINE: USING INTUITIVE EATING AND MINDFULNESS TO STOP BINGE EATING 81
- WAYS TO REDUCE THE SPEED AT WHICH YOU EAT AND DRINK 84

CHAPTER TEN: SUPPORT SYSTEMS 91
- COMPONENTS OF A BED SUPPORT SYSTEM 93
- HOW TO BUILD YOUR BINGE EATING SUPPORT SYSTEM 94
- HOW TO MEET NEW PEOPLE 95
- BEING A SUPPORT SYSTEM 97

CONCLUSION 99

BONUS: BED RECOVERY MEAL PLAN 101
- BED MEAL PLAN 103
- POINTS TO NOTE FOR CHILDREN IN RECOVERY 104

Introduction

We can all agree that food is a source of life. It is also an expression of feelings, like love and joy. In almost every culture, hospitality is expressed by feeding people. No celebration or moment of grief is complete without food.

The use of food for reasons besides mere sustenance is normal and common. However, it becomes a cause for concern when feelings become closely tied to food, and the two merge into one. This all begins in childhood. When you were good, you got candy; when you were bad, you didn't get dessert. When you had an injury, you were offered food. And on and on it went until food became more than nutrition. It morphed into punishment, distraction, an act of love, and a companion.

Now, food is how most of us deal with our emotions. It has become a form of solace when we feel hopeless and powerless. The minute food becomes a preferred means of coping, we quit seeking and developing new ways to deal with stressful situations. Then the pounds pile on, reinforcing the lack of self-control. So, here's the cycle briefly:

1. Feel bad.
2. Crave food.
3. Overeat.
4. Gain weight.
5. Cue the regret and self-loathing, while mourning the loss of the last pair of jeans you could fit into.

A buddy of mine (let's call him Sam) used to be 25 pounds overweight. One day, he told me about a bingeing episode he went through after an argument with his wife. I asked him why he chose food to deal with his feelings, and he responded, "I didn't have a choice." We talked for a bit, and together, we came up with five other things he could have done instead of bingeing:

1. Meditate.
2. Take a walk.
3. Take a shower.
4. Play a video game.
5. Hang out with a friend.

Sam agreed that he could have done anything else to take his mind off food and properly process his feelings about their argument. Maybe you understand what it's like to be in Sam's shoes. Stressful moments come, and it feels like there's nothing else to do but eat. In this position, you give in to that urge because you're overcome by powerlessness. As you are drawn in by the food, you feel incapable of dealing with the overwhelming problems. So, you feel powerless. Well, here's some good news for you:

1. You are not powerless.
2. You are not alone.
3. There is a way out.

You want to get back control over your life. You want to reclaim your power, and you deserve some accolades for that. You've taken a significant first step by reading this book. It's a sign that you're no longer willing to let those cravings rule your life.

You can quit binge eating, and through the pages of this book, I will take you by the hand and show you how to retrieve your power. It may seem daunting right now. You may feel like you don't have it in you to brave turbulent situations and not even think of food. However, you can. As you read on, you will learn how to put your head back in control of your gut.

With this book, you will learn how to find the space between emotional distress and your urge to feed. You will also learn to explore your thoughts and get comfortable with them, even when they're not all daisies and rainbows.

By the end of this book, you will finally see your true self, and a clear path to making that version of you a reality. As you act on every piece of solid gold advice in this book, you will gradually become the best and highest version of yourself.

You'll be so in love with sculpting the life you prefer, that your binge eating days will feel like a distant memory or dream. Soon, you will have regained mastery of yourself.

This might look easy, but I must warn you that it will take a bit of effort and time. The good news is, this is day one of the rest of your life. It's an honor and a privilege to be a part of your transformation.

You've got this in the bag. Now let's beat this. Together.

Chapter One: Introduction to Binge Eating

Once upon a time, the word "binge" meant drinking excessively. Now it means excessive eating. For some people, bingeing is a harmless activity like a mere overindulgence or a dietary lapse. For others, it means a total or partial loss of control over the urge to eat. This problem affects a significant percentage of the world's population — and not just Westerners. Despite being such a common occurrence, however, many people have little to no knowledge about the issue.

- Must a binge be massive?
- Is purging unavoidable?
- Is this a lifelong issue?
- Does this mean that there's another problem?
- What kind of people binge?
- Why do people binge?
- Is it normal to overeat?
- How do I tell the difference?
- How can it be fixed?

To answer these questions, we need a complete understanding of what a binge is and is not.

Dictionaries today define the word "binge" as eating excessively or an overindulgence. This overindulgence is not uncommon as both men and women have experienced it. For some people, it happens every once in a while and does not affect the quality of their lives. For others, like Sam, it is a real problem that affects many areas of their lives. To understand the difference between binge eating and mere overindulgence, you must define both behaviors accurately.

Recognizing the importance of this clarification, scientists conducted studies on the experiences of binge eaters. Now, while no two personal experiences are the same, binge eating has two core characteristics:

- The amount of food consumed is excessive, even though it may not seem like it to an outsider.
- Binge eating comes with a temporary loss of control.

Do You Have Binge Eating Disorder?

Here's a straightforward questionnaire that will help you figure out whether you are a binge eater. As a disclaimer, I would like to say that this is simply a profiling method and not a substitute for a professional diagnosis. It would be best to answer each question truthfully. A simple "yes" or "no" will do. At the end of the questionnaire, I'll tell you how the scoring system works. Here goes:

1. I always determine my self-worth by checking my body size.

2. When I have a binge episode, it feels like I am stuck in a trance or under some compulsion while I stuff my face as much as possible.

3. I have an obsessive relationship with food, weight, and calorie counting.

4. Most times, when I binge, it's because I was triggered by an intense negative emotion like loneliness, depression, anger, and so on.

5. I binge more times than I would like to admit. I am guilty of eating absurd amounts of food in a short time.

6. I feel disgusted with myself after an episode. I become overwhelmed with feelings of worthlessness and hopelessness.

7. Once I start bingeing, I feel like someone else is controlling my body.

8. I have been on too many diets, and I have followed each one to the letter fruitlessly.

9. I do everything I can to ensure that my bingeing remains a secret. I can't have people discovering this part of me.

10. It is usual for me to start and give up on diets multiple times in a relatively short period.

11. I suffer weight fluctuations often in just a few months due to my inconsistent dieting.

12. I either quit a diet or follow it to the letter.

13. Whenever I discover a new diet, I feel a sense of control over my cravings and hope that I might actually get thin.

14. I hardly ever feel good about myself physically and psychologically.

15. I always reach a point in my diets where I am sure to quit because the rewards are not as much as my efforts.

16. I am depressed half the time.

17. I continuously seek validation.

18. I am confident that I would feel more comfortable if I were thinner. I know that others would love me more.

19. I breathe perfectionism.

20. I always feel under intense scrutiny by others. It almost feels like they are bound to find fault in whatever I do.

Scoring System: If a question is true for you, you get one point. Go through all the questions again if you need to and calculate your number of points. If it is 13 or even 12 points, there are many Binge Eating Disorder (BED) red flags popping up around you. It means nothing concrete. However, you might be suspended by a fragile thread over BED spikes. Pay more attention to your eating habits, so things don't go overboard.

If you hit 15 points or more, you are, more likely, a binge eater. Don't fret. You're here, and that alone is a good start. The point of this questionnaire isn't to make you scared. The first step to fixing a problem is to become aware of it. Thankfully, this is not a virus.

Characteristics of Binge Eating

1. We'll start with how you feel. The first few minutes of a binge is typically pleasurable, from the texture to the taste of the food. You feel overcome with intense joy; however, this feeling doesn't last long. Soon after, it disappears and is replaced by equally intense feelings of disgust as you continue to stuff your face. You might even feel repulsed by your actions, but you will continue anyway.

2. There's the speed at which you eat. Binge eaters do it very quickly. It's almost like a mechanical action, stuffing food into their mouth at an unhealthy rate. They barely even chew it, and might even take large gulps of water or a drink to move things along. For this reason, they feel full and bloated. Also, drinking a lot of fluids helps with the purging that is likely to come after.

3. You feel agitated. Do you wander around or pace incessantly during a binge? Do you feel like you're being overwhelmed with feelings of desperation? These are all characteristics of a binge. That craving you feel that pushes you to eat is the reason bingeing is also called compulsive eating. In that brief moment, your priorities shift, and all you can think about is obtaining food. Some people eat trashed food or food that belongs to another person, shoplifting, and other degrading behaviors.

4. You feel stuck in a trance. When you binge, you experience an uncontrollable urge to keep eating even when you're full. It feels like you're on autopilot, and you're just watching yourself eat without being able to do anything about it.

5. You keep it a secret. Binge eaters hide their episodes because of shame, and they can do this for many years. They do this by eating normally in the presence of people and then letting loose as soon as they are alone. Another is by being deceitful. A binge eater would go back for the leftovers or take the food into their bedroom to eat in private.

6. You experience feelings of powerlessness. The lack of control that occurs during a binge is one of its core characteristics. It is what draws the line between binge eating and a simple overindulgence. Some people lose control before they even take the first bite while others lose it while eating. Then, they suddenly realize that they did it again.

Some people who have binged for years don't experience that loss of control anymore. They claim it faded over the years, probably because the recurrence taught them the inevitable nature of their binges, so rather than fight them, they plan for what is, to them, an unavoidable binge.

Planning gives them a bit of control of certain aspects of the situation, like where and when the binge will occur. This planning leads them to believe that they're still in control. However, deep down, they know that if they were really in control, they wouldn't be bingeing. Besides, these people still complain of an inability to stop once they start a binge session. No interruption could stop them, whether a phone call or a knock on the door. The binge goes on right after the distraction is handled.

How the Binge Happens

From the kinds of food consumed during a binge to how often the episodes occur, among other factors, binge sessions differ from one person to the next; therefore it's difficult to define and even identify a typical binge. However, understanding these factors is an excellent place to start. Let's break down each one.

1. The duration and frequency of the binge. It used to be that your binges had to happen as often as once a week before you got diagnosed with binge eating disorder. This criterion has been criticized over the years because it means people with less frequent episodes are not as impaired. Even the twice-a-week binge eater could use help.

Today, clinicians ignore these kinds of thresholds when diagnosing a patient. To be diagnosed with binge eating disorder, your binges simply must be regular and interfere with the quality of your life or physical health. The importance of frequency can still be confusing because some people binge once in a blue moon. Does this mean they shouldn't be worried? How often does a person need to binge for it to become a problem? Does the secret lie in how long it's been happening, and how often it happens? Or should one be concerned only when it affects the quality of their life?

As I mentioned earlier, clinicians pay attention to impairment, as in how badly BED has affected your health or the quality of your life. The time spent during an episode varies according to several factors, an important one being whether the eater has intentions to purge afterward.

Research conducted at Oxford University revealed that binge eaters who vomit tend to have an hour-long episode while others who don't throw up have longer ones. Why does this happen? The former feels pressured to finish as quickly as possible to vomit and reduce the amount of food that gets absorbed.

2. The kinds of food consumed during an episode. A binge eater's choice of food depends on two factors:

- The quality of the food, which can range from sweet to filling
- Their feelings about the food

They usually feel the food is "fattening" or "dangerous." Binge eaters tend to go for foods they typically avoid. I would know. I used to be addicted to sugar, so when I started my abstinence, I discovered that I was also a binge eater. I ran back into the sugary arms of sweet treats every chance I got until I permanently kicked the habit.

If you have done a little research, you may have found that craving carbs drives binges. The truth is that the amount of carbs in binges is no higher than that found in typical meals. If you have BED or know a binge eater, you'd know that binges usually include cookies, ice cream, cakes, and so on. In other words, binge foods are sweet and high in fat. What it boils down to is the forbidden nature of the food.

3. The amount of food consumed. The size of a binge varies widely between people. Some people eat large amounts of food, as much as 16,000 to 21,000 calories per episode. Some don't eat as much. The most common number of calories consumed per episode ranges from 1,500 to 2,000 kcal. I know someone who ate a little more than 2,000 calories per incident, which is about the average calories some women need to consume every day.

Laboratory research agreed with these figures when people volunteered to binge and have the exact amount of calories they consumed recorded. This study revealed that one out of five binge eaters consumed a little over 5,000 calories, and one out of ten consumed over 6,000 calories.

There are massive binges and tiny ones, but the diagnosis depends on perspective. A small binge may not meet the broad definition of a typical binge due to its size; however, what makes it a binge is that the binge eater considers that excessive by their standards, and has general feelings of powerlessness.

4. The cost of food consumed. The amount I used to spend on food was the most significant expense on my budget every month, and as the years went by, it drove me deeper into debt. Binge eating is an expensive coping mechanism and can throw you into financial difficulties.

Binge Eating Triggers

1. Hunger associated with undereating. Some binge eaters, especially the anorexic or bulimic ones, tend to eat very little outside of a binge episode. This malnutrition comes with many unpleasant effects, as is expected with starvation. Setting strict feeding boundaries and eating minimal amounts of food creates a growing psychological and physiological pressure to eat, and once you give in, it becomes difficult to stop yourself.

2. Violating a diet regulation. There are binge eaters who are also on a diet, and a strict one at that. They are meticulous about their feeding habits, like what they should eat, when, how often, and how much. Breaking even one of these rules can send them straight into an episode, which leaves them wracked with guilt afterward.

3. Taking alcohol. Some people feel more likely to binge after a few glasses of alcohol. Alcohol lowers our inhibitions, making us less likely to resist instant desires and violate whatever dietary rules we put in place. For instance, a plan to have just one plate of salad will be happily abandoned for a whole meal and dessert after a few glasses of alcohol. Alcohol can make you underestimate how bad you will feel if you break your rules. Also, alcohol tends to bubble up emotions that can result in a binge episode.

4. Uncomfortable emotions. Nobody likes to feel bad, but feeling bad can take on a whole new meaning for people who see food as a means to cope. These emotions can trigger a binge episode, leading to

even more unpleasant feelings. Depression is a particularly potent trigger. Others are hopelessness, boredom, anger, stress, anxiety, tension, loneliness, and so on.

5. Unorganized time. The lack of order in a day leaves some people vulnerable to bingeing, which is why I usually emphasize the importance of a routine. This lack of order comes with unpleasant feelings like stress or boredom, some of the emotional triggers I mentioned earlier.

6. Spending time alone. Most binges take place in secret, so being alone puts you at risk of succumbing to the urge. When you are alone, you don't have to deal with the social constraints surrounding the bad habit, so you're likely to indulge, even more so if you're lonely.

7. Feeling overweight. This is an experience reported mostly by women. Men feel this way too, but it is very uncommon. However, for both genders, this feeling's frequency and intensity are more significant for those with an eating disorder. For these people, feeling overweight translates to being overweight despite their actual size. This feeling can trigger an episode.

8. An increase in weight. Some people react very badly to even the slightest increase in weight. Gains as small as a pound can cause an adverse reaction. If this person is prone to bingeing, they might either stop trying to control their feeding habits due to feelings of hopelessness or go on a diet–and we have seen the many ways that could go awry. You need to understand that bodyweight is never constant throughout the day and all through the week due to temporary changes in hydration, not fat.

The End of a Binge

Bingeing every day can elicit different reactions from different people. Some people simply regard the episode as mere indulgence, while some become overwhelmed with guilt, regret, and even disgust at the behavior. They might compensate for these feelings by exercising and maybe eating less, but that is usually the end of the self-recriminatory act.

The aftermath of an episode usually begins with positive feelings, instant gratification, and relief from the emotions that triggered the episode. The anxiety or depression seems to vanish, but only temporarily because not-so-positive feelings swoop right in. Hopelessness creeps in because they feel powerless against their urge to feed. Anxiety is also a common aftermath because of the weight gain likely to result from their habit.

This unpleasantness may worsen because of the physical effects of bingeing, like tiredness, stomach problems, weight gain, and so on. Some people get so afraid of these effects they take extreme measures to compensate for their bad behavior, which, oddly enough, usually leads to more bingeing.

Eating Disorders and Eating Problems

A good percentage of people who binge don't suffer from an eating disorder because their binge sessions happen very rarely, don't physically harm them in any way, and don't affect the quality of their lives. However, if they perceive bingeing as an issue for them, then it is precisely that: An issue. Other binge eaters do have an eating disorder because it affects their physical health and the quality of their life.

There are three eating disorders experienced by teenagers and adults:

    1. Bulimia nervosa.

    2. Anorexia nervosa.

    3. Binge eating disorder.

Bulimia Nervosa

Also called bulimia, this is a major, potentially lethal eating disorder. A bulimic person binges uncontrollably on large amounts of food and then purges to prevent themselves from ingesting more calories than they feel they need.

To rid themselves of these excess calories and prevent piling on the pounds, bulimic people lean towards laxative abuse, enemas, self-induced vomiting, supplements for weight loss, and so on. Other ways through which they get rid of the calories and prevent weight gain are excessive physical exercise and strict dieting.

Signs You Have Bulimia Nervosa

1. You are obsessed with your body size and shape.

2. You live in constant fear of gaining weight.

3. You have recurrent bingeing episodes.

4. You feel overcome with powerlessness during a binge like you can't help yourself.

5. You force yourself to purge after a significant incident by exercising excessively or vomiting.

6. You make use of diuretics, enemas, or laxatives when you don't need them.

7. You restrict your calorie intake or don't eat as much outside a binge.

8. You depend on herbal or dietary supplements excessively for weight loss.

Anorexia Nervosa

Anorexia sufferers usually have dangerously low body weight, a distorted body image, and an intense fear of packing on the pounds. Anorexic patients are obsessed with controlling their shape and size, which leads them to use extreme methods that negatively impact the quality of life.

To prevent themselves from even the smallest increase in weight or simply continue losing weight, anorexics place severe restrictions on the quantity of food they eat. They use various methods to control their calorie intake, like abusing laxatives, inducing vomit, diuretics, enemas, or diet aids. They are also prone to excessive exercising, and no matter how much weight they lose, they don't feel satisfied.

This eating disorder isn't simply about food. It is a life-threatening and disturbing coping mechanism for emotional problems. With anorexia, self-worth equals thinness.

The physical symptoms of this disorder are remarkably similar to those of starvation.

Sometimes it can be challenging to notice the symptoms because low body weight differs among individuals, and some anorexics might not appear to be extremely thin.

Signs You Have Anorexia Nervosa

1. You have an abnormal blood count.
2. You are unable to make the expected developmental gains in weight.
3. You suffer an extreme loss of weight for your body type.
4. You feel fatigued.
5. You suffer fainting now and then.
6. You appear thin.
7. You have insomnia.
8. Your fingers look discolored and blueish.
9. Your hair is thin and often falls out.
10. You have soft, downy hair all over your body.
11. You have irregular or absent menstruation.
12. You suffer abdominal pain and constipation.
13. You cannot tolerate the cold.
14. You have low blood pressure.
15. Your skin looks dry or yellowish.
16. You have arrhythmia (irregular heartbeat).

17. You are often dehydrated.

18. You have eroded teeth from always inducing vomit.

19. You have swollen arms and/or legs.

Chapter Two: Meet the Nine Myths

Countless myths surround the situations and factors that encourage binge eating and what a BED diagnosis means. The only ways to dispel these myths are acceptance and understanding from the public, time, and more studies.

Popular Binge Eating Myths

Myth #1: Every binge eater suffers from obesity. This must be the most widespread myth about binge eating. Obesity does not equate to Binge Eating Disorder. Some plus-sized individuals are picky eaters, while some skinny people make pigs of themselves once a meal is in close range. Nom nom.

Bingeing does not always lead to obesity because fat distribution and storage are different for people. It's like assuming that everyone who wears dark glasses does so because they are blind. You might eat a burger, a bag of chips, pasta, and ice cream, and not add any significant weight. However, someone else can have a slice of cake and put on 5 pounds. Binge eaters with average weight still suffer the same negative feelings as obese binge eaters. The spotlight should be on the disorder, not necessarily weight.

Myth #2: Binge eaters possess zero willpower. Willpower is not as cut and dried as a slice of Iberian ham when it comes to BED. It isn't as easy as you think. As with all bad habits, your willpower is outmatched. Think of BED as a wrestling competition in which your plate always emerges the decorated champion. The diet-binge pattern is incredibly challenging to break.

Binge eating is an ingrained habit. The binge eater turns to food to soothe their uncomfortable emotions or get through a stressful day, even when they know it brings trouble. Again, if you're a binge eater, none of this is your fault. It ultimately boils down to the relationship society has with food, and how this affected you as you grew up. Binge eaters might have substantial willpower, but they also need techniques, support systems, and tools to get rid of this bad habit.

Myth #3: BED isn't a real thing. How does one chuckle on paper? Hahaha? Because this one's funny, to be honest. If that's true, you might as well trash his book now. Before binge eating disorder was an official thing, many couldn't understand how it fit into the class of eating disorders. So, clinicians and professionals had to define binge eating, emotional eating, and compulsive eating as **EDNOS**, which means Eating Disorder Not Otherwise Specified. But my oh my, how far we've come.

The game changed in 2013, when the Diagnostic and Statistical Manual of Mental Disorders, 5th edition (DSM V), classified binge eating as an eating disorder for the first time. Thus began the de-stigmatization of people who were dealing with BED. Today, EDNOS is called **OSFED** (Other Specified Feeding or Eating Disorder).

Myth #4: All any binge eater needs is diet, some discipline, and Bob's your uncle! Let's reread this myth for "clarity," shall we? Absurd does not begin to describe this suggestion. A diet is the last thing to do for BED. The diet-binge pattern is one of the critical traits of binge eating and a sign of the all-or-nothing mentality that puts binge eaters in trouble. While it's helpful to see a dietitian who will recommend a healthy and well-organized diet plan, binge eaters should stay away from weight loss diets.

Myth #5: Weight loss surgery can fix binge eating. Before I address this myth, I'd like to openly point out that I am not a doctor or health professional. I cannot and will not totally dismiss weight loss (bariatric) surgery as bogus. Positive statistics exist from people who have undergone such procedures, but I recommend that this option is approached with caution and only as a last resort.

Like I mentioned earlier, weight gain doesn't equate binge eating disorder. So losing weight after a bariatric procedure doesn't guarantee BED is gone forever. Surgery does not address the underlying reason you binge.

Statistics put forth by the American Society for Bariatric Surgery states that 40 to 80 percent of excess weight is lost between six months to four years, post-op. However, many patients still do not reach their body weight goals. Even worse, about 70 percent of the individuals who undergo any of the procedures usually regain some or most of the weight they lost post-op.

Could this be from suddenly being allowed to eat all the yummy snacks forbidden until three months after the procedure? Or the fact that you always feel hungry seconds after feeling full? Yeah, that's possibly your brain taking time to adjust to your cinched-in stomach. Before going under the knife, weigh the medical indications against the procedure's costs and risks.

Myth #6: All binge eaters are women. Statistics have shown that women may be more vulnerable to eating disorders. The media and social culture pressure them to look a certain way. This negative idea of body perception predisposes them to have unhealthy relationships with food and feeding. However, BED cuts across gender more than people are willing to believe.

About 45 percent of compulsive eaters and binge eaters are male, with figures seeming to be on the rise. Men are late bloomers in this regard. They look to food for comfort much later in life than women. However, regardless of gender, the experiences are mostly the same. Men might be unlikely and even reluctant to accept the existence of this disorder in their lives.

Myth #7: Binge eaters are always hungry. Bingeing and emotional eating have absolutely no connection to physical hunger. Every eating disorder has little or nothing to do with food or eating, ironically. Food is simply the coping mechanism or weapon of choice. When you binge on Ben and Jerry's after a crappy day or particularly painful break-up, does this mean you are starving? No! Does this mean the answers lie at the bottom of the ice cream tub? Well, that depends on who you ask.

Chronic binge eaters feed with no regard for physical hunger because it has become a self-soothing tool for any negative emotion. For treatment to be effective, you need to understand your reasons for bingeing to find healthier coping mechanisms for your feelings. Unfortunately, you cannot get through life without feeling bad now and then. Long story short, emotional hunger differs greatly from physical hunger.

Myth #8: All binge eaters are adults. You rarely find children diagnosed with binge eating disorder. They're kids, right? However, the alarmingly high rates of obesity in children today suggests that these little ones are at risk of developing **BED** when they grow older.

This phase of bingeing does not include the period of puberty when your children need their "beauty calories" to support their changing bodies. Children put on weight and even become obese for several reasons, but an important thing to know about children and eating disorders is that you cannot treat the child without treating the family equally.

Myth #9: Binge eating experts must be medical doctors. Your medical doctor should be your go-to for health problems that can arise because of BED, but your doctor is unlikely to have the expertise and time to deal with all the aspects of your treatment for BED. Binge eating is more mental than medical, so in conjunction with your medic, you might need a psychiatrist, psychotherapist, and even a dietitian on speed dial. Working closely with these professionals who have knowledge and experience with this behavior will help you cope better with BED.

If you have been a binge eater for a long time, the odds are that you feel like a lost cause. It's even worse if you are overweight, spend a better part of your life looking to change your habits and shape by criticizing yourself, embark on strict diets, use laxatives to induce vomiting after every binge, and so on. It isn't easy living in a fatphobic society where you get flack for not having "enough willpower" to change.

You don't even have to be fat to feel fat, especially with the resounding message that you are unattractive and unacceptable. You have been in a battle with your gut for as long as you remember. You think you will be accepted once you shed those pounds, so you spend years struggling through the motions of many fad diets in an unhealthy effort to look or seem the way society insists you should look. Well, we will change that, starting now.

A Shift in Perspective

The first thing you need to do is change your perception of your inability to lose weight. Look at it as your refusal to submit to the discriminatory boxes you should check before you finally have the "perfect body." This way, you grow to love yourself as you are, warts, boogers, and all. From this strong position, your motivation to lose weight is from a place of self-love, not self-loathing.

Think about all the times you have attempted a diet and ended up bingeing. You binged because you focused on the symptoms, not the disease itself. Every time you tried to claw your way out into the light, you found yourself right back where you started. Your body became your own worst enemy, refusing to lose the habit and the pounds. This refusal, on some level, represents your rejection of the discriminatory culture that governs us today. It also means you insist on using food to escape, your go-to, feel-good drug, until you no longer require it.

Cultural conditioning is deceptive at best and damaging at worst. Ten people could eat the same thing, expend fairly identical amounts of hours of physical activity, yet still end up with different body sizes. Fitness protocols abound everywhere you look, from pop-up notifications on your screen to billboards with models who have undergone so much airbrushing they bear a resemblance to creatures from outer space.

Cellulite, laugh lines, stretch marks, wrinkles, and thick thighs are bashed, criticized, and hidden. In contrast, thigh gaps, gravity-defying breasts, humongous behinds, six-pack abs, and fully toned limbs are praised and desired. You'd think we possessed the power to force our bodies to distribute fat in a certain way. This culture makes you repeatedly question your image in the mirror. Full cheeks make you scream. A slight jowl or waggle under your chin makes you pinch yourself, hoping your face will get the memo. Imagine the degree of shock the folks from Da Vinci's era would feel if they somehow found a way to make a trip to the future.

Today's world makes you feel like crap because you have consistently refused to give up your attachment to food while refusing to feel good about yourself. You crawl even deeper into your hole of self-loathing and condemnation because you think you're a failure.

Your lousy habit may seem like a way to display an unwillingness to embrace cultural discrimination, a culture you have unknowingly internalized. Like a marionette, you suffer a pull from opposing sides.

At this point, your arms, if not your mind, must hurt like hell. What's with the food shaming anyway? If food and fat are so bad, why do they exist in such delicious forms? Why does fried bacon smell better than boiled broccoli? This is an honest question, not an excuse for you to abandon healthy fruit and vegetables. So, because you habitually foster negative emotions, you compulsively want to drown in more negativity.

Let go of one of the ideals. Pick between you and the notions in your head. Sometimes, this choice isn't always natural. However, I promise with a high degree of certainty that making that choice changes everything. I am here to help you with a plan that ensures you live a healthy life without using food as a coping mechanism. You will improve at identifying your triggers and dealing with your emotions so there won't be a need for the 'fix' that is food which only leads to the 'pay-off' that is fat, both of which do nothing but abandon you to feelings of guilt and regret after every binge.

Two Prongs of the Problem

The first issue is your emotional triggers. The second is your tendency to run to food for comfort instead of your thoughts for solutions. We all want the magic pill, that cure-all that would reduce if not eliminate all the reasons that have us making a beeline for that cookie jar, the fridge, or the Hershey bar.

I have to be candid with you: Problems never end. Emotions can stay unaligned or out of equilibrium for an extended period. The good news is, you need not solve all your problems or line up your emotions like pieces on a chessboard to quit bingeing. It is, in fact, the complete opposite. You need to revisit your relationship with food.

Start with thinking long and hard about why you need to eat to feel better about yourself and the situation at hand. This helps you avoid the mindless eating that comes hand in hand with unbalanced emotional states. Face those problems head-on, like the boss you were born to be.

You can begin by recognizing and addressing the real issues that trigger you. Does dieting help? Not really. Think of diets as a band-aid on a gaping sore. Pus still leaks. Which means you must confront the real demons sooner than later.

One of the crucial skills you must learn to beat this habit is identifying and distinguishing real hunger from emotional hunger. To do this, you need to recognize real hunger for what it is: The physical desire living beings have for nourishment. You have to respond to those signals instead of lumping that desire together with emotional discomfort. Food, which you perceive as the enemy, is the key to transforming yourself into a person you can face every morning, a person who can think through and solve their problems.

Phantom Hunger

When you get hungry, how exactly do you feel?

- Does it grow slowly, or does it hit you like a train out of nowhere?
- Do you feel desperate to eat something immediately?
- Do you mind having any nutritious food, or is there a particular kind of food in mind?
- When you finally eat, do you pay attention to the food going into your mouth, or do you stuff your face with it?

If the hunger hits you like a train, makes you desperate to eat not just anything but something in particular, and you bury your face in it when you do eat, then that isn't physical hunger. This peculiar craving is called phantom hunger, and it's the culprit responsible for your binges.

I like to regard binge eaters as having two stomachs: one physical and the other, phantom. The hunger you feel in your stomach (the real one) is a signal for you to eat. That part is biological; you need to feed to survive. If that's the only hunger you respond to, you don't belong to the binge eating club.

The phantom stomach is where the problem lies. This stomach, which doesn't even physically exist, has roaring pangs of its own. It gives you a signal to feed it when you experience uncomfortable situations or emotions. It is the more demanding and persuasive stomach of the two. Think of it like stuffing a lot of paper down a pipe to stop water from coming through. Eventually, the paper gets soaked and soggy.

Chapter Three: BED and Body Weight

Binge eating disorder is linked to various challenging situations. With time, they turn your healthy, happy life into a sad and frustrating one, affecting your relationships with others. BED also affects your physical health (as you probably already know), and this either results directly from overeating or unhealthy weight control practices.

Most of these health issues are reversible, while some are not. Most even become worse as time goes on. I recommend you nip them in the bud as early as you can.

Before we get into any of that, there are some points I would like to discuss about "body weight." This discussion is needed to clarify the many misconceptions surrounding the term.

Key Facts About Body Weight

As I mentioned earlier, most binge eaters have an almost obsessive concern about their shape and weight. Despite the attention given to this aspect of their life, many still have internalized misunderstandings about weight. Let's clear all of that up.

- We consist of mostly water. As an adult, roughly 60% of your body weight is simply water. Let's say you weigh 150 pounds. The amount of water in your body weighs about 90 pounds. Facts like these could be the one trick to helping you sleep better at night. Those cyber-bullies mocking your fat arms? Pfft! Don't fret. Biology says it's water, and last time I checked, it is healthy to stay hydrated.

- Our body weight is not constant all day, every day. These weight fluctuations are short term and usually very negligible, ranging from 1 to 2 pounds. They are mostly a result of changes in our hydration. Because we are 60 percent water, little changes in our hydration levels have a noticeable, yet negligible effect on our weight. For binge eaters who purge or abuse diuretics, their hydration levels are continually changing due to the loss of water from these practices. The result is a considerable change in body weight.

- Some weight changes are short term and have nothing to do with changes in body fat. As I mentioned earlier, weight changes are usually the result of changes in the body's water content. Remember this each time you get on the scale and see that you are down a number. Your body fat is fine, don't check the internet. No, it is not a medical condition. Our weight yo-yos sometimes. I can't stress this enough - stay, hydrated!

Quick Facts About Weight Loss and Dieting

There are many people with binge eating disorder who are gravely worried about their diets. You might be guilty of this too, with your nose buried in articles and books on nutrition and diets, possibly because this makes you feel adequately informed. Maybe these books satisfy your craving for knowledge, but a lot of health professionals agree otherwise since many of these diet plans are unreal. Just because a macrobiotic diet (or even worse, the baby food diet) helped your neighbor's cousin's boyfriend does not make it sustainable.

Many people have fallen prey to the tactics used by advertising and media companies. These companies sell you thoughts, ones you digest a little too well. These thoughts, in turn, shape your ideas so you catch yourself cringing when you see someone who eats with gusto. Your eyes develop calorie counters over something as healthy as a plate of quinoa salad.

What I am saying is that many people hold a ton of misconceptions about weight acquired through years of internalizing information from inconsistent and unrealistic sources. Here are some key facts about weight loss and dieting:

1. A single healthy diet doesn't exist. A diet is healthy when it matches the nutritional needs of the individual. It ensures optimal health subjectively so that as your dietary needs evolve, your diet stays adaptable.

For many adults, especially the elderly and middle-aged population, a healthy diet constitutes foods that reduce the risks of heart disease, cancer, and weight gain. However, this is not the optimal diet for pregnant and lactating women in the same age bracket. Specific meal plans also exist for people with certain health issues like chronic inflammation, diabetes, etc. So you see, a "perfect" diet is a fairy tale with unicorns and sphinxes.

2. Diets for weight loss are not particularly healthy diets. Diet plans with weight loss stamps on them have one function and one function only — to assist people in losing weight. They are not necessarily healthy or sustainable, even with the promise of helping overweight individuals achieve a healthy weight.

These diets work by creating an energy imbalance in your body. This way, the calories gotten from food or drinks are less than the calories that your body needs to function. The imbalance makes your body turn to fat as an alternative source of energy to survive, and if sustained, helps you shed some pounds over time.

The question now is, at what cost? Between persuasive marketing strategies from supplement companies, diet cults, pyramid schemes, self-proclaimed gurus, and our natural desire to be perfect, we adopt the most extreme diets only to suffer health issues after attaining the ideal weight. My advice? Stop taking diet tips from media outlets. They are out to get you. Literally.

3. Diets for weight loss are strictly for overweight or obese people. If you don't suffer from obesity, you don't need a weight loss diet. Unless you want to achieve a body mass index below 18.5, think twice before signing up for a weight loss plan.

Do not let the love handles you got after thanksgiving dinner ruin your self-esteem. A body mass index below healthy weight has physical, social, and psychological side effects you will not like very much.

4. Weight loss diets change with the tides of fashion. Whatever is trending this year, may not be in style next year. For instance, carbohydrates were frowned upon in the 60s and 70s; then dietary fat became the bad guy in the 80s and 90, and carbs were cool again, till they suddenly became the enemy again in the 2000s. Once upon a time, it was the in-thing to be waif-like and stick thin. Now, the curvier, the better. On and on, like moving trains, these trends will come and go.

5. Weight loss differs from weight maintenance. Weight-loss diets are not to be used for a long time because they don't consider your nutritional needs. As I have mentioned repeatedly, some of these diets are certain to harm your physical health if sustained for the long term.

Realistically, only a handful of people can religiously stick to a diet for over six months. After that, it becomes critical. There is always a tendency to quit and go back to old diet habits. This makes one regain all or most of the weight lost. Doubtful? Try facing a pan of sizzling, stone-baked pizza after being on a keto diet for two months. Nothing tests your patience as much. The solution I would recommend is more straightforward and less brutal on your digestive tract.

Maintain your current lower weight instead of striving (and failing) to shed more pounds. To do this, you must switch from thinking weight loss to a weight maintenance mentality. This point, often omitted in weight loss programs, is the biggest culprit in why so many participants eventually regain the weight.

6. A healthy diet should have a large variety of foods and plenty of water. The only things to keep to a minimum are sugar, saturated fat, trans fat, and salt. Saturated and trans fats increase our risks of heart disease, type II diabetes, and stroke. The World Health Organization estimates 500,000 to be the number of deaths from trans fats each year. That should be enough information to steer clear of the cookies, pies, dairy creamers, and frozen dinners.

Saturated fats can be found in dairy and red meat, while trans fats can be found in fried foods, many commercial pastries, and hard margarine. However, not all kinds of fat are dangerous. Unsaturated fat helps reduce the risks of cardiovascular problems. Excellent sources are seafood, olive oil, fish, nuts, and others.

The confusion, however, lies with how to turn these healthy guidelines into real eating habits. How should you eat? Health educators made use of a food pyramid to illustrate the appropriate portions for each class of the food. Today, they use a plate instead of a pyramid (www.choosemyplate.gov).

The reasoning and guidelines remain the same; only the approach and perspectives differ. Food pyramids are so fourth grade. With the healthy plate method, you are stuck with a pattern easier on your belly, your health, and, more importantly, your memory. It is one method that encourages mindful eating, as you already know how to load up each quadrant of your plate.

7. It is better to obtain vitamins and minerals from food. Vitamins and mineral supplements in the form of liquids or pills do NOT

replace actual food. Yes, sometimes, supplements may be advised following prescription by a health professional. Still, your body is smarter than you give it credit for. It synthesizes and regulates an adequate amount of vitamins and minerals required for your survival, and it is wise to let it do what it does best. If you feel like you suffer from nutrient deficiency, consult a health professional.

8. Perfect eating habits are unnecessary for ideal health. If you are worried about perfection in your diet routine, I want you to know that it isn't required. You don't have to weigh your dry oats on a scale to make them fulfill your ideals of portion control and balanced eating. Guidelines for a healthy diet are just guidelines. The beauty of guidelines is they can be adjusted and adapted to every individual, so feel free to be flexible.

Body Weight and Binge Eating

Obesity means different things to different people. A person suffering from anorexia will define it as any gain as small as two pounds. The average older adult may think they are obese because they weigh 167 pounds on their large-boned muscular body. In the fashion world, being obese might mean being 5"10' with a bodyweight of 135 pounds. It is absurd that the passport to strutting down a glamorous runway in impossibly high heels (or flats) is to look like a wafer.

None of these people are obese by medical standards. If anything, anorexic people and some models are way below a healthy weight. I say some because there is more inclusive modeling now. Different people have their own opinions about body mass. There are people concerned about a few pounds while there are those who don't mind a few pounds.

From a medical standpoint, an individual is obese when their body weight is about 20 percent more than the healthy weight for their age, body type, and height. An individual is morbidly obese when their body weight is more than 100 pounds above the healthy weight stated for their age, height, and body type. Today, there's room for a few more pounds per height in the "fit" weight bracket than was initially proposed.

Present-day BMI has a bit more wiggle room to accommodate weight gain due to several factors linked to an imbalance between energy intake versus energy expenditure. Compared to before, technology has made a lot of things easier. The result of everything being a button or click away is a sedentary lifestyle. This ease, coupled with living in the big city, has contributed to more opportunities for consumption while dramatically reducing chances for physical activity.

Some studies conducted by the CDC a while back revealed that about 60 percent of American adults are medically above a healthy weight. Among them, 36 percent are only moderately overweight, while the rest are obese. Results from the research revealed that about 12 percent of children living in America are grossly obese.

Another government-funded research released in 2002 discovered that 31 percent of America's entire population is grossly obese. It also showed that the number of people between the ages of 6 and 19 who are obese is approximately 15 percent.

Let's assume that those statistics are a little outdated. More recent studies have shown that about 35 percent of female American teenagers and 25 percent of teen boys are moderately overweight, with 13 percent of boys and 16 percent of girls being downright obese. What could cause these appalling numbers? That's a whole other kettle of fish–and maybe a completely different book–to be honest.

Why are Millennials battling weight? There's a myriad of reasons, from fast food, colorful, cheap, and strategically placed snacks with ridiculous amounts of sugar and fat, the fast-paced life, the curse of instant gratification, and binge eating. BED is the cause of the obesity spike in so many areas of the world.

Chapter Four: Binge Eating and Science

If your goal is to prevent BED, you will need to accept, identify, and understand the cycle of binge eating to extinguish its influence. Also, if your goal is treatment, you need to repeat this process to discover why BED has such a cult following and pinpoint the chief factors that keep BED alive.

The Biology of the Binge

Data collated by the Organization for Economic Cooperation and Development (OECD) in the year 2017 shows that obesity is becoming a massive problem in America, Colombia, Mexico, New Zealand, Hungary, and some other countries. What this means is that people have become victims of their food lust.

Over time, scientists have found a connection between appetite and hormones. The discovery of two hormones, ghrelin and leptin, has changed the face of nutrition. These two hormones regulate hunger.

Binge eating is greatly influenced by factors including behavior, socialization, immediate environment and, not surprisingly, genetics.

If intense enough, there are specific life changes that affect our levels of hunger biologically. Look at it this way: If you feel terrible, you're more likely to wholly or partially lose your appetite temporarily. This behavior is in stark contrast to the way you treat food when anxious. With anxiety, for the most part, you tend to overeat when surrounded by certain sights or smells that have been hunger triggers for you in the past.

The rise and fall of your hunger levels are usually affected by a string of precisely set up signaling mechanisms intensively studied in psychology and neuroscience.

Binge eating isn't just physiological. It has strong ties to certain psychological factors, such as the mysterious world of behavior and emotions. Thousands of people who battle BED do so because of low self-esteem and a low sense of self.

These issues are rooted so deeply that many researchers have dedicated their time and energy to figure out the reason this part of the human makeup isn't an easy fix. Don't you wish the choices were more relaxed, limited to-you know-choosing whether to stuff your face today or not? To eat or not to eat, dear friend, remains the question on our minds today.

Scientists today have discovered several methods through which humans mentally process health and illnesses. This process is multifaceted and all-encompassing. Thankfully, today, there is increased awareness concerning the factors that make people prone to bingeing. These factors include hormonal involvement (leptin and ghrelin), genetics, energy levels throughout the day, early life, parts of the brain responsive to certain smells and sights, etc.

On Leptin and Ghrelin

Leptin and ghrelin are the two hormones that significantly influence your metabolism and energy levels. Like yin and yang, where leptin moderates the balance of your energy and induces weight loss, ghrelin gives you hunger pangs.

People suffering from obesity have increased leptin. The more they eat, the more fat stores they have, hence more leptin. Scientists have proven that obese people are leptin resistant.

George Snell and his colleagues discovered genetic involvement in obesity at Jackson Labs in 1950. The word "leptin" is from the Greek word leptos, meaning thin. In 1966, Douglas Coleman and his colleagues isolated the leptin gene. Jeffrey Friedman cloned the gene artificially following some parabiotic experiments in 1994. This discovery, isolation, and artificial synthesis became the nirvana of obesity research.

Leptin is released into the bloodstream by adipose tissue stores in the stomach, heart, skeletal muscles, and placenta. This hormone can cross the blood-brain barrier–a selectively porous membrane protecting your brain and neurons from toxins or pathogens that cause infections. Leptin levels are affected by your degree of physical activity, age, gender, and glucose uptake.

Ghrelin, discovered years after leptin in 1999 by Masayasu Kojima and colleagues, did not receive as much fanfare. This does not affect its importance. The word "ghrelin" was coined from a Proto-Indo-European word ghre, which means "to grow." Originally thought to exist only in the stomach lining, advances in research have proven otherwise, isolating the hormone in areas such as the adrenal cortex, digestive tract, ovaries, and pancreas.

Like leptin, ghrelin is influenced by gender, age, body mass index, glucose uptake, levels of growth hormones, and insulin. Ghrelin is present at high levels before you eat and after you fast. The only time this hormone cuts you some slack is when you eat. This is the reason diet-induced weight loss is not sustainable long term. As well as affecting your sleep cycle, ghrelin also affects the amygdala, which is the reward center in your brain. This is why the more hours you sleep, the less ghrelin you have, and vice versa.

These two hormones make a mess of brain signals in obese people. The reason your body isn't cooperating with your new diet, fancy exercise regimen, and all the other steps you have taken to ensure an ideal body weight, is that your brain is, biologically speaking, confused. With binge eating, you are stuck in this vicious cycle:

- Eat when the hunger pangs come knocking.
- Pack on the pounds when no one's looking.
- More leptin gets stored in fat tissues.
- Confusion in your brain from stunted levels of leptin signaling.
- Your brain's hypothalamus sends a desperate cry for help.
- You succumb to your body's need to eat.
- Soon you get hungrier.
- You eat and pack on even more pounds.
- Rinse and repeat.

With leptin resistance, your brain throws in the towel. It stops acknowledging the signals sent by this hormone. This thick skin your brain has grown is the leading cause of obesity today. In simpler terms, your leptin levels are through the roof, which means you are obese, but your brain cannot detect this.

With leptin resistance, obese men and women store fat differently. Men store more visceral fat (hence that beer belly), while women have more subcutaneous fat (under the skin) in different areas.

All that body fat muddles your appetite signals to make you hungrier. It happens to everyone sometimes. You are here because it happens to you a little more often than "sometimes," and that's okay.

Binging and Brain Functions

The spotlight does not belong to biological makeup and basic anatomy alone. Research has shown that bingeing is a kaleidoscope of brain functions, acting together to influence feelings, behavior, psychology, and thought processes.

This approach is in dispute with specific theories famous among other binge scientists. They would instead shift the blame for bingeing to some meticulously selected neural networks, pathways, and hormones. This method simplifies an otherwise complicated process, unrivaled for a long time in the history of science. It is the logic behind many scientific achievements as it has been used to identify, simplify, comprehend, and provide viable solutions to many food-related illnesses.

However, there are some natural occurrences and tendencies that go against the grain. These factors defy human or scientific laws and hypotheses. These laws are founded on our limited comprehension of the situation. The human body is not an electronic device or smartphone possessing faulty parts that are easily identifiable and blamed for their shortcomings.

On a scientific level, bingeing results from hunger based on cravings and the feeling of being unsatisfied, as implied by the amounts of ghrelin, leptin, and dopamine released by the brain. BED goes beyond being a system requiring investigation. It is a disorder that is almost intentional, but not exactly. It results from a glitch in some chemical transmission mechanisms in the brain and body.

When you feel hungry again right after you just ate, very complex sequences of chemical signaling and feedback loops happen to produce the unsatisfied feeling you are experiencing. When you feel satisfied, this doesn't mean that your stomach is necessarily about to overflow with food. It is just your body responding to your current dopamine levels, glucose, and several other hormones sent out by your brain to let you know to stop eating.

Let's explore this a little further. Insulin, a hormone created in your pancreas, regulates the amount of sugar in your blood. Unfortunately, certain people cannot make this hormone due to a faulty pancreas. These people have a medical condition called type 1 diabetes. There is another blood sugar disorder called type 2 diabetes. Here, there is adequate insulin. However, the body cells are not quick to pick up this vital hormone.

When your body fails to process blood sugar properly, adipose tissue (fat) begins to form. Your body interprets the unstable levels of sugar and the recently deposited fat molecules as signs that the individual isn't satisfied despite having just eaten.

From all you have just read, you can see how easy it is for our bodies to tip this delicate balance. There are so many factors that share the blame. If not, binge eating disorder, diabetes, and obesity levels wouldn't be so high. Issues with work, personal relationships, loss and grief, stress, and aging are other factors that influence our metabolism, rendering us vulnerable to this imbalance.

Psychological Factors That Sustain BED

BED has certain psychological factors that sustain and even worsen it. Let's look at a few:

You can't help your feelings of disgust and regret. Two words familiar to every binge eater because of how often they are used and felt after an episode are disgust and regret. This feeling has different forms. It could be the feeling of overwhelming shame that envelops you when you practically inhale three plates of chips and salsa.

How frequently do binge eaters feel like this? These feelings depend entirely on how often the episodes occur. Frequent bingers feel this way after almost every food-related incident. The intensity of these feelings grows when you fall off the wagon after attempting yet another diet plan. As a binge eater, you turn to diets not only to shed pounds but also to create a sense of control over your seemingly uncontrollable cravings. This diet provides you with short-lived relief before the illusion wears off. This leads to the "crash" that forces you to confront the feelings you have successfully avoided for a few weeks or months.

You are afraid of your inability to stop. You know that feeling of hopelessness and despair in your gut when you feel trapped or stuck? That is BED toying with you. Once you develop this doom and gloom mindset, you reinforce its hold on you.

You finally surrender to your reality of munching through your worries only to feel horrible after. You grow reliant on bingeing to help you work through problems that could be solved if you looked up from your plate long enough to analyze and work through your issues mentally.

You equate weight with self-worth. You feel unworthy because you believe that you are just not thin enough.

You live by strict rules of perfectionism. Dealing with a binge eating disorder comes with a massive amount of self-consciousness. This most likely stems from the assumption that people see you the way you see yourself–perfect when you are skinny, a loser when you weigh an extra pound.

With BED, you raise the bar too high and never acknowledge your wins no matter how great they seem. The most appropriate way to describe a typical binge eater is a person who demands only perfection from themselves but is always lacking in confidence, constantly expecting themselves to fall below their unreasonably high standards.

They have a this-or-that perspective, sorting their life experiences and thoughts into black or white boxes, leaving little to no space for any other angle. This thought pattern is so dominant it can be passed down through generations in families.

This perspective is an unforgiving, toxic way to see things, and it is not particular to BED. With this view of life, you become more prone to binge eating, seeing it as a means to ease your guilt or desperation. This behavior does not manifest magically overnight because you have binge eating disorder; instead, it is a trait you already had ingrained long before BED made an appearance. Your life is not a silhouette of black and white. You need a pop of color, a middle ground that allows you to love yourself regardless of your imperfections.

You tend to seek validation from outsiders. This is one behavior that is almost automatic to everyone with BED. You know the drill: Asking questions like "Do I look fat? Do you think I have lost some weight?" This line of questioning shows your desperation in seeking outside opinions, whether you are aware of it or not. This behavior creates a lack of trust in you and yourself, eventually crushing whatever little self-esteem you were holding onto. People-pleasing is another one of those behaviors that existed before your eating disorder. It merely became amplified by BED.

You don't plan any of your meals beforehand. If you don't plan your meals, you throw yourself into a situation where you must buy food impulsively, which gives a lot of room for emotional decisions. If you feel negative emotions or intense hunger, you're likely to lose control. If the week ahead promises to be busier than usual, take some time out during the weekend to map out your feeding plan.

Cook some tasty meals and store them in ready-to-go plates. Declutter your fridge and do away with junk food. This way, you won't reach for a bag of crisps when you have had a bad day.

You ignore your cravings. We can't argue about the importance of a healthy, well-rounded diet. The mistake most of us make is ditching sugar. The more you deny yourself the things you want, especially when they're so easily accessible, the more you desire them. It'll do you better to face your cravings head-on. However, instead of bingeing on so many bags of chips, it is advisable to call a friend and go out for a nice cup of ice cream.

Cheat days are totally acceptable, and as you will later learn, so worth it. Too many cheat days becomes a problem. That fitness guru you have been following for months on Instagram has days when he'll pig-out and lie in ratty t-shirts instead of yoga wear on his couch. You can even make a planned event out of this, a whole day to satisfy whatever cravings you may have — just one day.

You tend to eat and multi-task. Research has proven that mindful eating (which I will explain in detail shortly) is a holistic treatment that produces lasting results for people with binge eating disorder. A particular study noticed that binge eaters, who regularly engaged in mindful behavior, developed an awareness of their eating habits and went from bingeing four times a week to once a week.

Mindful eating has helped more people with eating disorders than you can imagine. Take my friend, for instance (let's call him Jake). Jake has confessed the wonders of mindful eating after reading several self-help books on rediscovering the joys that come with savoring food.

His practice of mindful eating may have started as a remedy for BED, but it grew into something that stayed with him. Now he is fully aware of his emotions and physical states, which help him distinguish between phantom hunger and real hunger.

I am not suggesting that it is possible to stay conscious of your feeding activity, especially when you completely lose control while doing something else like texting or watching a movie. What I am saying is that change is possible once you are aware of your habits. To do this, you need to be present in mind, body, and soul when having your meals.

You don't sleep enough. Neglecting or cutting corners around your sleep makes it difficult for you to deal with BED. Getting enough sleep is an essential aspect of good physical and mental health. Besides going to bed late, habits like working in your bedroom or using electronics in bed can affect your beauty sleep. Remember what

I said about ghrelin levels reducing when you sleep? Imagine the sky-high levels of this hormone that exist when you work on your laptop at 3 am. By that time, you join the exclusive fridge raiders club, scouting your fridge, cabinets, and other hidey holes for treats.

You skip breakfast often. There are some widespread misconceptions about breakfast that need to be nipped, like how it speeds up your metabolism so you lose weight like magic. That isn't true. The truth to that myth, however, is that a full and healthy breakfast provides you with enough energy for your day-time activities. This way, you are not prone to snacking as much as you used to. These two changes punch **BED** right in the face, so endeavor to squeeze a healthy breakfast into your morning routine. You will thank yourself at the end of every day.

You tend to choose workouts you do not enjoy. Engaging in physical activities helps curb the urge to binge. Many people think that workouts must be intense to help with weight loss, which usually leads to them giving up. Rather than engaging in a routine you don't particularly like, engage in some physical activity you enjoy doing.

You forget to relax and have fun sometimes. Play-time does not end because you are "adulting." Your options are broader than that available to a toddler in kindergarten. Forgetting to participate in fun and pleasurable activities can stunt your efforts to curb your eating disorder. Playtime is an essential aspect of **BED** treatment, mainly if it guarantees quality time with people who love and support you. A healthy social life keeps you from falling into a depressive lifestyle likely to trigger bingeing. Relaxation is very relative. There are days when the most relaxing thing you can do is an activity that can be done alone, like taking a walk or checking out the thrift store. On some other days, you want to go hiking with some friends in some unexplored area. There isn't a one-size-fits-all activity for relaxation, so do what works for you.

You are very secretive about your disorder. **BED** brings a type of shame that is difficult to shake. Some people have admitted to feeling like freakshows because of their eating disorder. This feeling is understandable. Fighting these feelings is not a solo journey. You'd be surprised at how understanding your loved ones can be if you gave them a chance. Have a conversation with someone you trust and tell them all about what you go through. You can call them in moments when you feel hopeless and lonely.

Chapter Five: Physical Effects of BED

Dieting

There are serious health hazards attached to dieting. Research has proven that yo-yo dieting, which is the recurrent cycle of weight loss and weight gain, changes body metabolism and composition in ways that make it more challenging to lose weight in subsequent attempts.

Effects of Food Deprivation and Unhealthy Weight Loss

More studies have shown a link between individuals with weight fluctuations due to excessive dieting and cardiovascular disease. The risk of death by heart disease is high in people who diet excessively. Dieting is more dangerous than many people realize because unnecessary weight loss and food deprivation have many psychological and physical health hazards.

1. You become extremely sensitive to cold, including suffering from cold hands and feet.

2. Your sleep cycle suffers, and you experience sleep disturbances like waking up earlier than is typical for you or often during the night.

3. The bladder loses strength. You pass urine more frequently than you're used to.

4. Body hair growth skyrockets. Those pesky hairs that spring up in places that are usually bare. For example, chin and chest hair for women.

5. You experience poor blood circulation and a weak pulse, which can lead to fainting spells.

6. The bones become very thin, which can cause fractures and even deformity. Case in point: osteoporosis where your bones lack calcium and phosphorus. These two minerals contribute to the strength of the bones. Osteoporosis is not to be confused with Osteogenesis imperfecta (also called brittle bone diseases), which is genetic.

7. Menstruation becomes irregular or ceases altogether.

8. The stomach reduces to an unnatural size. It feels uncomfortably stretched after eating a tiny amount of food.

9. You experience recurrent and frequent constipation.

10. Anemia because the bone marrow where the white and red blood cells are manufactured starts to malfunction.

11. Liver damage from malnourishment. This condition causes a deficiency of body proteins and swollen legs and ankles.

12. Unusual spikes or increases in the level of blood cholesterol.

13. You suffer overall fatigue, which can lead to paralysis or muscle weakness.

14. There are stunted growth and delayed puberty in younger people.

Physical Effects of the Binge-Purge Cycle

The binge-purge cycle is a familiar occurrence with certain eating disorders such as bulimia nervosa, anorexics who binge, and some individuals with binge eating disorder. Not surprisingly, inducing vomit has several adverse effects. These effects are common with individuals who have done it repeatedly and frequently for a while. These effects range from mild to severe as you will see in a bit:

- The teeth suffer damage. Frequent and repeated vomiting causes extreme damage to the teeth. The inner surface of the dental enamel gradually erodes. The gingival tissues lining the mouth can deteriorate, leading to mouth sores. The patient could also suffer from a dry mouth, a medical condition called xerostomia. Dental fillings remain unaffected but may become pronounced relative to the surface of the dental enamel.

Since vomit contains stomach acids that erode the tooth enamel, dental decay stops once the vomiting stops. The damage is irreversible but not degenerative. Brushing your teeth immediately after throwing up or rinsing the mouth with water after vomiting works to accelerate decay and tooth sensitivity rather than prevent it. The rationale behind delaying brushing or rinsing is because the gastric acids produced by your stomach lining need some time (at least an hour) to settle down. Oral care performed immediately after causes the acids to sink further into the enamel, aggravating dental decay.

- The salivary glands swell. There are three main glands in the mouth responsible for producing saliva. They are the submandibular, parotid, and sublingual glands. Of all three, the parotid glands are the most affected. Parotid glands, located behind the mouth, above the jaw, and beside the ear, are only visible when severely inflamed.

This condition is common with individuals who vomit regularly and on purpose. Swelling is generally painless, but saliva production increases two-fold. Parotid gland swelling gives the sufferer's face a chubby and rounded appearance. Because the cheeks are typically inflamed, the symptom is termed "chipmunk cheeks."

These individuals see their round faces and assume that their entire body must be rounded and fat as well. This physical condition increases their worry about their weight and shape, making the eating disorder even worse. The swelling is reversible and slowly goes away once the vomiting stops.

• The throat suffers damage. The most common way of inducing vomit is manually stimulating the gag reflex. The most common method of stimulating the gag or pharyngeal reflex is sticking your finger down the back of your throat. Your finger touches the back of your tongue and the area around your tonsils.

This action causes the tell-tale spasms that force food or other substances out of your oral cavity. This process can be long and complicated, and sometimes requiring more force which causes superficial wounds to the back of the throat. These wounds cause a lot of pain when eating and talking and are prone to infections. Hoarseness, recurrent tonsillitis, or sore throats are quite common.

• The esophagus suffers. Violent vomiting can rupture the esophageal walls (the muscular tube connecting your mouth to your stomach), but this is an infrequent occurrence. Repeated vomiting increases the risks of esophageal rupture (called Mallory-Weiss tears), requiring immediate medical attention. Frequent vomiting puts you at risk of inhaling vomitus. This condition predisposes you to upper respiratory tract infections and weakens the muscles at the base of your esophagus, leading to a condition known as Gastro-Esophageal Reflux Disease (GERD). If you notice fresh blood in your vomit (a condition medical professionals call hematemesis), please seek medical help immediately.

• The hands are at risk of damage. This is another side effect of manually stimulating the gag reflex with your fingers to induce vomit. It is very damaging to the skin of the fingers, particularly the knuckles.

The first abrasions to appear on the hand are due to the friction between the hand and the incisors. These abrasions, known as Russell's sign, are named after their identification and description by Gerald Francis Morris Russell, a British psychiatrist, following his 1979 publication on Bulimia Nervosa.

- There is a significant imbalance of fluids and electrolytes. The physical effects of repeatedly inducing vomit can be life-threatening. These effects are especially true for people who try to "rinse out" their stomachs by drinking water and inducing vomit until the vomit runs transparent, free from food particles. Vomiting by itself affects hydration and electrolyte levels, so constant vomiting can leave a person severely dehydrated.

The most disturbing kind of electrolyte imbalance is called hypokalemia, which means low levels of potassium. This condition can cause potentially lethal heartbeat irregularities (arrhythmia). If you notice you have an irregular heartbeat, seek medical advice immediately. Some signs that you have electrolyte or fluid imbalance include dizziness, fatigue, lethargy, swelling of the extremities, extreme thirst, muscle spasms and twitches, and so on.

Although people who frequently go through the binge-purge cycle usually have some electrolyte and fluid imbalance, most experience no symptoms. Those who do show symptoms of electrolyte imbalance are affected mildly. It is also crucial to understand that other health problems can cause these symptoms; thus, they aren't always indicators of an underlying electrolyte and fluid abnormality.

Electrolyte imbalance is reversible, ceasing when the vomiting stops. It rarely requires medical attention by itself. Any treatment for electrolyte imbalance should be supervised by a medical professional. Never attempt to treat it on your own. A small number of individuals induce vomiting with chemicals and other emetics. For instance, they can drink very salty water to make themselves throw up. This is very dangerous and another cause of electrolyte imbalance. Others use over-the-counter medication to induce vomiting–an equally harmful practice.

Physical Effects of Laxative Abuse

Some people with binge eating disorder take laxatives to control their weight by controlling food absorption through purging. This practice is not as common as self-induced vomiting. Some people take as many as 60 to 100 laxative pills at once. Yikes! They probably don't know that no matter the number of laxatives consumed, laxatives don't have as much effect on food absorption as they think.

Laxatives act on the lower digestive tract, while food absorption occurs in the upper part of the gastrointestinal tract. Watery feces are produced instead, leading to a drop in weight because of the water loss. Remember what I said about water making up 60% of our body weight? The weight loss may be noticeable, but it is very short-lived because there is weight regained after rehydration. Nevertheless, these people consider this weight loss very rewarding because they believe it is proof of the laxative effect on food absorption.

Laxative abuse, like self-induced vomiting, comes with dangerous electrolyte and fluid abnormalities and symptoms similar to those I mentioned earlier. People who abuse laxatives and also induce vomiting are at increased risk of malaise.

Certain laxatives can wreak permanent damage to the intestine when used for long periods and taken in high doses. The physical effects are generally not irreversible because people who engage in this practice regularly can become properly rehydrated in a week or so if they discontinue use immediately.

Going cold turkey will lead to temporary weight gain, which can be very worrisome for some. Many laxative abuse victims cannot cope with the side effects of quitting this habit, pushing them right back into the arms of their laxatives. This is why people need to understand that weight gain is a side effect of hydration, not food, and it will disappear in a matter of weeks.

Physical Effects of Diuretic Abuse

Like laxatives, diuretics cause you to lose water, but unlike laxatives, they work by causing excessive urination. This weight loss is short-lived because there will be weight regain following rehydration. When consumed regularly and in high quantities, diuretics can cause electrolyte and fluid imbalance, both potentially lethal, yet reversible if discontinued immediately. Like laxatives, diuretics can cause individuals to experience temporary weight gain after quitting them.

Physical Effects of Excessive Workouts

Brutal exercise is another unhealthy practice binge eaters get into. They might exercise excessively to alter their weight or shape. These strenuous workouts start out great initially.

Binge eaters never notice the damage they are doing to their bodies until they become severely underweight or suffer muscle injuries due to overuse. For anorexics who are also binge eaters, some exercises are hazardous because they can cause bone fractures.

Physical Effects of Having Low Body Weight

Many people are not aware of the adverse effects of being underweight. People can look healthy and still be underweight because their weight in relation to their height, age, and body type is inadequate. Being underweight is one effect of binge eating disorder, and it has the following physical consequences:

1. It affects the brain. Underweight people have significantly reduced grey and white matter in their brains. Dieting makes things worse because our brains need energy. When this energy is restricted or in short supply, our brains do not function properly. All those kilos you plan to lose to fit in can lead to a low blood count. The red blood cells (hemoglobin) carry oxygen to the brain to aid its function. When you are malnourished, hemoglobin is in short supply, starving your brain of nutrients needed for cognitive abilities.

2. Blood circulation suffers. Being underweight has adverse effects on the heart and blood circulation. The heart muscle undergoes

atrophy, resulting in a weak heart and inadequate blood supply to the rest of the body. Blood pressure takes a nosedive, and the heart rate significantly reduces. This puts the sufferer at an increased risk of developing arrhythmia, heartbeat irregularities, especially when accompanied by electrolyte and fluid imbalance. If you have a heartbeat that is less than 50 beats per minute or irregular, consult a doctor immediately.

3. Hormonal imbalance. When underweight, the body goes into survival mode to keep you alive. In survival mode, the body conserves energy by ceasing all nonessential functions, including producing certain hormones. This imbalance results in reduced production of sex hormones, affecting mostly women because they become infertile. Men are not left out either. A disruption in hormonal equilibrium can lead to decreased overall body hair and erectile dysfunction. For either sex, libido, or sexual responsiveness, takes a nosedive as well.

4. Brittle bones. Being underweight can and will significantly impact bone strength. I do not have the slightest idea of how the breatharians do it, but your body needs calcium, phosphorus, and zinc to build strong bones and teeth. With malnutrition, there is a significant reduction in bone strength. This side effect is partly due to hormonal changes and partly because of the decrease in body weight. The bones are not under any pressure to bear your body's weight anymore. As a result, they get weaker. Conditions such as these put patients at a high risk of fractures and osteoporosis.

5. Impaired digestive system. Underweight patients may experience a persistent feeling of hunger, although this is not a common occurrence. The taste buds suffer reduced sensitivity, which leads people to turn to large amounts of spices and condiments for flavor. The gut begins to work very slowly, probably to maximize food absorption. Food stays in the stomach longer than usual, because a decreased metabolism implies that it is moving very slowly through the small intestine. This explains why underweight individuals feel full even after eating very little.

6. Loss of muscle strength. Besides the loss of bone strength, there is also muscle weakness or wasting. This condition is called atrophy. Muscle wasting results in increased feelings of lethargy in performing activities that would have been easy for you to handle if you were at ideal body weight. Loss of muscle strength is most prominent when trying to get up from a squatting or sitting position, or climbing the stairs.

7. Poor skin and hair condition. This effect is different for different people. Lanugo, a form of downy hair, may grow on the abdomen, arms, face, and back. There may be a significant loss of hair from the scalp. The skin usually gets dry and has an orange hue like a lousy tan.

8. Poor temperature regulation. The body experiences a significant drop in temperature resulting in chills, especially in the hands and feet.

9. Poor sleeping habits. Sleep is also greatly affected, with a high chance of frequently waking up earlier than usual.

Physical Effects on Pregnancy and Fertility

The link between binge eating disorder and fertility problems is still unclear for several reasons. Dieting, being underweight, and general weight loss affects fertility beyond a doubt, but research is still underway to confirm if binge eating alone influences reproductive capacity. It is essential to note that these effects are not irreversible and can be fixed once the eating disorder is treated.

Similarly, there isn't much known about the link between binge eating disorder and pregnancy. The majority of the studies conducted on eating disorders focused on bulimia nervosa. However, social experiments show that binge eating reduces significantly when a woman realizes that she is pregnant. The urge to quit this habit is borne out of a strong desire to protect her unborn child, thus successfully preventing binge eating throughout the pregnancy. The use of laxatives and self-induced vomiting declines significantly. Some pregnant women might binge due to dietary cravings, not negative emotions.

Around the second trimester going forward, many women with BED tend not to worry so much about their appearance or weight. This is because they no longer hold themselves accountable for the body changes-as they shouldn't. They recognize these physical changes are inevitable and should be embraced.

Others choose to binge until they can binge no more. This tendency to stuff their faces full because "the baby needs it" doubles their risk of increased weight gain, leading to complications during pregnancy and delivery. It also means they will have more weight to lose after childbirth.

On the flip side, there are pregnant BED sufferers who fear any form of weight gain. So, they exercise hard, diet heavy, and sometimes turn towards laxatives and induced vomiting. This vicious cycle results in little or no weight gain, but their babies might be under weight or suffer neural tube (brain and spinal cord) defects. Underweight babies, in particular, are at risk for potential long-term consequences.

Chapter Six: Loving Yourself

Body Image Problems

Struggles with body image is a critical factor in the binge-purge cycle. On this journey of healing, you owe it to yourself to understand the root of these distorted body images and how the majority internalize them.

The media and the fashion industry. Countless studies have x-rayed the role the media and the fashion industry play in creating and sustaining these distorted ideas of the perfect body in the western world. From a very young age, we are flooded with images of people who are unnaturally thin and "perfect." These photos are usually heavily photoshopped, leaving us to internalize these unreal slim bodies that are impossible to achieve as our body goals.

The number of people signing up for cosmetic surgery and other make-over programs is on the rise, creating and reinforcing the illusion that plastic surgery solves the "'appearance problem." Your nose seems too long? Fix it. Want a smile brighter than the flash of your camera? Get veneers. The muffin top that would have disappeared after a few months of exercise and healthy eating is nipped and tucked to perfection. This only promotes the idea that everyone needs to conform to the dictated concept of beauty, which in reality changes every decade.

More men seem to be jumping on this wagon of unrealistic beauty ideals, leading to increased negativity about their appearance. This negativity hits the roof even more after going through fashion magazines, body pornography, or advertisements on TV. This has led some countries to issue government bans or guidance against this, like banning the use of impossibly skinny models or trying to educate the younger generation to create awareness about body positivity.

Then there are social media. The scourge of the present generation. The compound where a massive chunk of our time is spent. A virtual universe where 'likes' seem to equate value. Some people have no idea that individuals with a strong online presence are usually carefully managed. About 60% of users take time to edit their selfies before uploading them, altering their skin tone, removing blemishes, or even reducing body size. This culture only leads to unhelpful and unhealthy social comparisons where you sink even deeper into that pit of self-hate.

Fat talk: Ever heard the term before? Maybe that beautiful friend of yours with clear skin talking about her breakouts and having to take extra care not to "ruin her face even further." Another classic example, after a major exam in school, the star student whines at great length. Her dull monotone consists of her being worried she might fail. It is called humble bragging and is a habit practiced more by women compared to men. It results in making the other party feel very inadequate. However, it is challenging to tell these people to quiet down because they sound seemingly humble.

There are other variations of this, like a friend whining about how terrible she looks when she actually looks gorgeous and most likely knows it while assuring you of how great you look in an outfit you don't feel good in. The classic example happens when two people talk about how a person shouldn't be wearing certain outfits at their age, weight, or social standing.

This might seem harmless and like innocent small talk to the people who partake in this behavior, but it is hurtful and makes victims feel terrible about themselves and their appearance, even more so if the recipient of this behavior has an eating disorder.

Cons of discriminatory attention and comparison against other people:

A study on binge eating disorder was conducted, with volunteers being a combination of people with and without **BED**. They were shown pictures of their bodies and the bodies of others and asked to point out the ugliest and most beautiful body parts. While they did this, assessments conducted using eye-tracking technology were used to measure how long and how often they looked at the beautiful and ugly parts.

People with **BED** lingered more on their so-called ugly body parts and less on the ugly parts of others, while volunteers without **BED** had their gazes fixed on the more beautiful body parts belonging to others. People with **BED** pay discriminatory attention to aspects of themselves that they don't like and tend to be harder on themselves than others. This self-criticism reinforces bad eating habits because judgments like these make them feel a variety of negative emotions.

The harsh self-criticism leads them to believe that others see them as they see themselves. It is not uncommon to see people affected by **BED** complain bitterly about how this unfair discriminatory attention against themselves affects their lives and relationships with others.

Now more than ever, self-love is a prerequisite for happiness. Society and our mirrors do not make living easy. If your image behind a piece of painted glass gives you so much grief, worry no more. Science need not prove what we already know — that mirrors are not the best judges of what we look like because they distort the same image they reflect.

Excessively checking the body and seeking reassurance. There are people with **BED** who spend unreasonable amounts of time assessing the body parts they dislike, checking it again and again from several angles. They spend an obscene amount of time measuring different body parts, especially those they do not like. This obsessive behavior is unhelpful and unhealthy. It is sometimes accompanied by continually seeking validation from others about their appearance.

There are others, however, who totally avoid eye contact with their body. Some even go as far as hiding all the mirrors or looking away when they are naked. You might wonder how body checking, avoidance, and continuously seeking validation is terrible, considering it doesn't really harm anyone. Although it reduces unhappiness and anxiety about your appearance for a short period, after a while, all these feelings come rushing back worse than they felt before. Having gone this far with the book, let's examine the connection between negative emotions and binge eating.

Become Acquainted with Your Body

1. Shut your eyes and touch your body gently. Start with feather-light touches and slowly feel your way into a caress. Begin with your face and move slowly downwards.

Get a good feel of all your body parts on your way down. How does it feel beneath the pads of your fingers? Does your skin feel smooth or rough, cold, or warm? Do you feel your heartbeat beneath your palm? Do you feel your rib cage expands as you breathe? Do you feel comfortable touching your skin or does it feel frightening and unpleasant?

2. Now move to a wall and stand up straight with your back straight, your head and shoulders pressed firmly against it. How does that feel?

3. Walk around the space like you are proud of your appearance. Keep your head upright, but ensure that you don't overstretch your neck or head.

4. Pick any slow song you like and move your body gently to the beat. Now change the song to something upbeat. Dance like nobody's watching.

5. For this part, begin with a body part you like. Touch this part gently, apply some oil, and softly massage it. Now expand the area and do this until you have rubbed down everywhere your hands can reach.

Taking Care of Your Body

- Ensure you get enough quality sleep.
- Make a list of things to do for or with your body that you know will make you feel good. You could take a walk, sunbathe, dig the garden, swim, get a haircut, dance, soak in a bath with essential oils, go to the spa, and so on.
- Relax now and then. It is an excellent way to rejuvenate the mind and body.

Extra Helpful Tips

- Managing avoidance, constant validation-fishing, and body checking. Observe and note how often you do these things and the time you spend doing them. Draw up a plan to reduce these figures as gradually as is comfortable for you. If you have a habit of continually seeking reassurance from a particular friend or loved one, talk to them and let them know not to give you the reassurance you seek because it is unhealthy and the effects are short-lived. You can tell them to remind you of the time you told them not to reassure you. They should hug you or do something you'd prefer instead.
- You need to accept and be kind to neglected and less-liked body parts. This exercise requires you to picture that body part you don't like; your tummy that you wish could develop washboard abs, your big thighs, or square jaw. Now you will write a letter to yourself from those body parts. Let them tell you how they feel, what they do for

you, and how they assist other body parts in taking care of you. Give them a chance to speak.

• Accepting the cause of your body image issues. Do you know if the negative perceptions you have concerning your body are related to experiences from your past, like your cousins making fun of your shape or weight? Were you bullied at home or school?

When you figure out the cause of your self-hate, the first thing to do is write a letter to whoever traumatized you all those years ago, and tell them what they did and how they made you feel. Now write a letter to yourself as a reply from them. Apologize to yourself as if coming from them.

Finally, write a compassionate and comforting letter to your younger self, the one who experienced all those horrible things. If you could speak to that person, what comforting or reassuring things would you say? Write it all down, and go over all the letters. How do they make you feel?

Learn to Live with Your Body

I have a friend. Let's call her Sally. Now, Sally called me late last summer to tell me she had come up with an idea to deal with her body image problems and I thought it was brilliant. She compiled a list of things she would usually avoid because of her appearance, writing them down in a hierarchy, beginning with the things she avoided the most and why, down to the things she avoided but feared least. This list is precisely what she showed me during our bi-monthly dinner.

• Going to the beach or swimming in a bikini. Practically impossible.

• Slow dancing with any man. I find it unbearable to get that physically close with anyone.

• Attending a party, I fear meeting new people because I wonder what I would talk about. I have always been scared I might run out of steam and become the third wheel in everyone's conversations.

- Going to a restaurant with family or friends. How will they see me after watching me eat?

- Wearing a tight skirt. I am insecure about the size of my stomach and waist.

- Dressing up in short sleeve outfits, I have flabby arms.

- Dressing in brightly-colored clothing, I have always felt that only parrots, piñatas, and gummy bears should be that bright. I don't like to draw attention to myself.

It takes steel guts to pen your fears down like that and give yourself a timeline to smash them like you are ticking off tasks on a to-do list. Compile a similar list yourself and tackle them one after the other at your own pace. You can start with the easy ones this week and slowly progress into the more difficult ones. These tasks should be on your schedule for the week, under weekly goals. If you decide to give this a shot, don't expect it to be a walk in the park.

Sally told me in confidence that she had panic attacks when she went bikini shopping. Her face was so red. Her heart seemed to stop for a whole second. The shop attendant had to get her ice cubes in a paper towel to steer her mind away from the fear. I would advise you to remain open to difficulties and anxiety. You will need to ease into it.

10 Celebrities and Eating Disorders

Eating disorders affect many people, including the seemingly untouchable stars. Underneath the glam, smiles, and rose-colored glass disposition we see on the red carpet, they are very human and go through just as much as everyone else. Let's look at what they had to say about their recovery.

1. Demi Lovato: Pop star and X factor judge, Demi came forward about her issues with her appearance and her recovery from an eating disorder. In Ashley Graham's podcast on February 19, 2020, Demi spoke of her battle with body image and self-love from the age of three, which progressed to compulsive eating at age eight.

Demi suffered from bulimia as a teenager and started cutting. It was so bad she ditched her tour with the Jonas brothers in 2010 to seek professional help. In addition to scoring her skin, she battled with feelings of shame and bipolar disorder. Like many of us, Demi always compared herself with Instagram models online.

In her words, "I admit that I have come so far physically, emotionally, and I have never been prouder of my progress today. Looking back, I feel sad for having treated myself so harshly when I was younger. I strongly believed that I should look like everyone else, but over time, I realized beauty comes from within and it comes from accepting who you are. When I started caring for my soul, mind, and body, I learned that I needed to conform to no one's idea of normal. Slowly but surely, I started to love myself."

2. Melanie Chisholm: This star, popularly known as Sporty Spice, spoke about how motherhood helped her on her journey towards healthy eating habits and self-love. She said, "When I was a member of the Spice Girls, it was so stressful always being in the spotlight, and this led me into a toxic relationship with exercise and food. It was an obsession. By the year 2000, she suffered from anorexia, BED, and depression, all in a bid to become the "perfect" Spice Girl.

She said, "I was worried about everything that I ate, and I let go of a lot of food groups, like protein and carbohydrates. I lived on vegetables, fruits, and very little else. When I realized that I was pregnant, I knew almost immediately that I had to do better, I had to be healthy if I wanted to give Scarlet the nourishment she needed to grow strong, fit and healthy."

3. Paula Abdul: The singer, former American Idol judge and present judge on the show So You Think You Can Dance revealed her 15-year battle with bulimia. In an interview with People Magazine, she admitted to extremely long workout sessions, which led her to binge eating. "I always had my head down the toilet, spitting out my food and feelings." After getting professional help, Paula admits in her words, "There are three things that I must do every day. Do an hour-long exercise, never skip any meal, and accept the shape and size that I was created with. I had times when I just sat down and said to myself, "You're feeling regret about what you just ate, and it's unhealthy. Stop it!"

4. Jane Fonda: This star has been very open about her struggles with bulimia that lasted for multiple decades. In a tell-all essay to Lenny Letter, she spoke of her father's role in her eating disorder. He would send his wife at the time to tell me to "lose weight and wear longer skirts."

She also admitted to three of her stepmothers having the same struggle with food, possibly a side effect of being married to her famous actor father. One of her numerous stepmothers told her all the ways she would have to change her body if she wanted a boyfriend. "I was not what you'd consider happy from puberty until age 50. It took me a lot longer than most. I was in my 40s when I decided to make lasting changes to my mental and physical health. Bulimia gets worse as you age because it takes longer to come back from an episode. My entire life was at stake. I knew I needed to choose whether to live or not."

5. Snookie: Popularly known for her participation in Dancing with the Stars, Snookie revealed her problems with anorexia many years ago. She said, "Cheerleading was the highlight of my high school experience, but I wouldn't say it was always easy. I started to fall into anorexia. We had these little female freshmen showing up who weighed about 70 pounds.

At the time, I thought my spot on the team as a flier was in jeopardy, so I resorted to starvation. I would have just one plate of salad a day, which progressed into one cracker daily, then one grape, and soon, I would go without eating a thing for about three days. It was an absolute nightmare for me."

6. Stefani Joanne Angelina Germanotta (Lady GaGa): At a young women's conference hosted by Maria Shriver, GaGa spoke about her teenage years, her struggle with bulimia and anorexia since the age of 15, and how she longed to be a skinny ballerina but could not make it past being a curvy Italian little girl who gorged herself on meatballs and pasta every night.

Lady GaGa embarked on a project in 2013 (the Body Revolution), where she created a section on her website with unedited photos of herself. She encouraged her followers to share their so-called imperfect pictures, so they could learn to accept themselves.

She said, "My weight fluctuations since I was young have bothered me to no end. I believed there was no amount of help that could make the pain go away. My boyfriend loves my curves, so he always encouraged me to eat right, stay healthy, and not worry about my appearance. I am more at peace than I have ever been, and I will not put myself at the mercy of scrutiny ever again. I am proud of my body no matter the size, and I love you all and would like you to be proud of your form as well. "

7. Zoe Kravitz: The actress who played an anorexic character in Road Within, (2013), later spoke up about her 10-year struggle with bulimia and anorexia. She said, "I went through some difficulties around 16 to 18 years old." Zoe claims she felt a lot of pressure not only from being in the spotlight as the daughter of the famous Lisa Bonet, but also from constantly being surrounded by supermodels when she was with her dad Leonard "Lenny" Kravitz.

Teenage years already come with insecurities, and for her, this was the icing on the cake. She once revealed in an interview with the July issue of British Vogue Magazine, "My eating disorder started in high school, and as such, had little or nothing to do with fame. It was more about being a woman, the perfect woman. I felt under so much pressure."

8. Russell Brand: Brand revealed dealing with binge eating and bulimia as early as age 11. "It was an unusual thing and very embarrassing because I was a boy, but the feeling was euphoric. For me, it was more about isolation and getting out of myself. I liked feeling unpleasant and inadequate." He sought professional help and can boast of being clean now, with a better-looking plate, body, and mindset than he did as a teenager. However, he admits it was a bumpy ride.

9. Troian Bellisario: The Pretty Little Liars actress revealed that she became anorexic due to feeling pressured to do well in school. "I began to self-harm when I was still a junior." She once subjected herself to living on as little as 300 calories a day. At some point, she thought even that was too much to eat. "I simply wanted to make my parents happy and be a perfect girl to everyone.... I felt like if I opened up about my sadness or any negative emotions, they might disown me. I kept it all to myself and ended up being more self-destructive than ever." She has been in recovery for over ten years, she says.

Bellisario was so worried about her eating disorder she became terrified of motherhood. After she became pregnant with her daughter Aurora, she accepted the ups and downs of motherhood with the help of her support system–a team of women close to her. The 2017 movie Feed written and produced by her and directed by Tommy Bertelsen shows her playing a teenager with an eating disorder who struggles to pick up the pieces of her life following her twin brother's death. She admits this is the first time she confronted her past issues with food on the big screen. The movie script helped her understand her past better. Talk about turning a struggle into an art form. Way to go, Bellisario!

10. Evanna Lynch: The Harry Potter actress, fondly called Luna "Loony" Lovegood was born the third out of four children to schoolteacher parents, surrounded by farm animals growing up. Evanna was diagnosed with anorexia nervosa by age 11. She reveals it was her friend J.K Rowling who saved her. "I told her (J.K.R.) that her books kept me going, especially the character, Luna Lovegood. I told her that I really admired her. She actually wrote back and became like a counselor to me. She showed me that anorexia is not creative but destructive, and I should be brave not to give in to it."

Evanna opened up to the Irish Times in 2016 about her eating disorder and how she spent two years in the clinic. She was very open about how letters written by J.K Rowling while she was in and out of the clinic helped her live again. She is a healthy weight now.

Chapter Seven: Intuitive Eating

In this chapter, I am about to share a diet that isn't a diet. Picture a meal plan that allows you to eat whatever you want when you want it, one that focuses more on wellbeing than on calorie intake and body weight. When I first came across the idea of intuitive eating, I breathed a heavy sigh of relief. Finally, a Utopian diet, I said.

Intuitive Eating (IE) and eating intuitively are not the same thing. Eating intuitively is an aspect of IE based on a method of eating. Similar to our feeding patterns as newborns, eating intuitively involves searching for food when we feel hungry or in need of some comfort, stopping the minute we feel sated or full. But when discussing Intuitive Eating, I refer to methods that help us build a healthy relationship with food.

Intuitive Eating is a paradigm or a set of principles for eating and connecting to food and your body. Resch and Tribole created this concept to help people who seem stuck in the binge-diet cycle and other eating disorders, helping them get reconnected with their natural feeding instincts. With this method, your decision on when and what to eat is strictly based on your body's requirements and satisfaction, not any external rules. Thousands of clinical professionals use this method today to help as many people as are willing to break the seemingly never-ending cycle of self-hate and bingeing, and encourage individuals to trust their body signals a little more.

Ten Principles of Intuitive Eating

1. Reject the diet mindset. To do this, you will have to get rid of all the diet magazines and books that promise you falsehoods of shedding pounds easily, permanently, and quickly. Assume dieting is not the answer. Like Elsa from the cartoon Frozen, you should "let it go."

2. Honor your hunger. Ignoring your hunger forces your body to trigger a primal need to overeat, snatching the control right out of your hands until it is satisfied. Once you switch to autopilot eating, all your intentions to eat moderately and consciously go straight out the window. Learning to acknowledge your biological cues is the first step to rebuilding the trust between you and your body.

3. Learn to make your peace with food. This principle requires you to call a truce and quit hating food. Stop counting calories. Allow yourself unrestricted authorization to eat. If you keep telling yourself things like, "I can't eat this," "I shouldn't eat that," you will most likely end up depriving yourself, which will develop into an uncontrollable urge, ergo, bingeing.

I will illustrate this by telling you the story of the Swedish monarch, King Adolf Fredrick. He was famous for his gluttony-binge eating. Remembered more for how he died other than how he ruled, King Adolf died after consuming an enormous meal in 1771 during the Mardi Gras festival.

This king had a feast featuring caviar, boiled meats, turnips, sauerkraut, champagne, kippers, and lobster. All that was just the appetizer and main meal rolled into one. For dessert, he ate not one, but fourteen Semla-a traditional Swedish dessert consisting of a cream-filled bun served in a massive bowl of milk flavored with cinnamon and raisins. He died of indigestion soon after. Binge eating is a sad way to go, but at least he went into the light with a full stomach.

When you choose to starve yourself for a long time, your body finally overrides your so-called rational thinking (because it will), making you eat with a scary intensity that will result in overeating. Your food then leaves you with guilt and overwhelming regret at best, and a torn esophagus and ruptured stomach at worst.

4. Confront the food police. Always oppose those thoughts that congratulate you on eating next to nothing and chastise you for eating a cookie. Never hesitate to put them in their place. Remind them (or yourself) that their style of choice is known as "nibbling," not eating. Seriously though, eating like a sparrow went out of fashion ages ago along with steel boned corsets and hoop skirts. Defunding the food police is a crucial step in rediscovering your natural food instincts.

5. Discover the pleasure factor. The Japanese take the art of beautiful food presentation seriously. They call it moritsuke. They believe that taking the time to plate a meal attractively has fantastic benefits. In intuitive eating, this is especially important, because seeing our food is just as important as consuming it. In a scientific experiment conducted on human behavior, participants in the research rated an aesthetically arranged plate of salad as tastier. They were intent on paying twice the price for it.

6. Learn to acknowledge your fullness. Ever heard the Japanese phrase "Hara Hachi Bu"? This phrase is an eating technique attributed to Confucius- Chinese philosopher, political figure, and teacher. The phrase loosely translates to "Eat until you are 80% full." Anything past the 80% mark is plain greed, no matter how we slice it.

With overeating, you get so full, pass out, or find yourself doing the number two for days in a row. If you are going to acknowledge your fullness, you need to trust yourself to give your body the nourishment it needs. Pay attention to body signals because your body has an inbuilt thermostat of sorts that gives you an unmistakable sign when you're full. Observe these signs and acknowledge them. If you're still learning to identify your body cues and meanings, don't worry, just stop in the middle of your meal, check how the food tastes, sip a little water, and then assess your current level of hunger.

7. Manage your emotions with compassion. The phrase "Kill them with kindness" works not only for bullies and nosey neighbors. It would help if you were kind to yourself and emotions too. The first thing you need to realize is that food restrictions and deprivation can mentally and physically trigger a temporary loss of control the same way negative emotions do.

Search for healthy ways to comfort, distract, resolve, and nurture your problems. Loneliness, anger, sadness, anxiety, and boredom are feelings experienced throughout life, each with its trigger and appeasement. There are many ways to do this and the key is finding a good distraction besides food. A new hobby will do.

8. Show your body some respect. Own your size, be it a size four or a size 16. Please don't go shopping for jeans that are two sizes too small. They won't fit you tomorrow, or next week. Even if they do, they will make your rear look like a crepe. You need to respect your body if you want to feel more comfortable in your skin. Rejecting the diet mindset (point number one) will be difficult if you remain unrealistically critical of your shape, weight, and size. Your body deserves some dignity and a much-needed break.

9. Focus on movement. Ditch the militant exercises and simply engage in physical activities that feel good. I am not saying you should chuck your Insanity Max 30 in the bin if you actually enjoy it. All I suggest is that you let your focus shift from burning calories to the feeling of simply being active. After a workout, you should feel energized, not drained. Look for an activity that helps you stay enthusiastic about your health and well-being. Not only that, but it should also keep you happy about shedding those pounds.

10. Honor your health with tasty nutrition. Let's be frank, wheatgrass and kale smoothies taste like piss and fermented mulch weed, even with blueberries. But, according to nutritionists and health buffs, it is chock full of antioxidants, vitamins, anti-inflammatory agents, immune boosters, and the power to neutralize toxins. Still, it's a bit of an acquired taste. Make food choices that honor your taste buds and your health, so you feel good all round.

6 Intuitive Eating Myths

Myth #1: Intuitive eating simply means eating cookies and hamburgers for as long as you live. This misconception is the most widespread and understandably so. When you have spent so much time avoiding certain foods, even if you binged on them during episodes because they are forbidden foods, you will desire them in the early stages of Intuitive Eating. It's called the "Honeymoon Phase."

During these early days, it feels like you will never tire of burgers, fries, cake, deep-fried Oreos, or whatever you termed forbidden. But the phase fades. Generally, the moment a food stops being considered a taboo, and you don't feel the need to deprive yourself of it anymore, it becomes just like every other food.

When that finally happens, it will feel more natural for you to eat a large variety of meals, including the forbidden ones. Many people retain that craving for cake, cookies, and the like, but they also start to genuinely appreciate and desire other kinds of food, including veggies and other healthy foods. I bet you wish you knew this earlier, or you could inject this knowledge like a flu shot into your kids' veins, especially if you are the parent that has to literally put on a carrot costume and dance around to make them eat their veggies.

On the flip side, this will probably seem like an unrealistic dream if you feel trapped in a never-ending binge-diet or binge-purge cycle. You don't think you'll ever let go of your cravings or the guilt you feel when you consume these seemingly bad foods. In reality, you feel an out-of-control desire for these things because you always deprive yourself of them. Ever heard the saying, "People want what they can't have?" Denying your body of particular foods makes them more attractive. The calorie deprivation following this denial makes your brain respond quicker to any food-related stimulus, especially the ones we consider more alluring. But the moment you quit the mental and physical deprivation, you recognize these foods as just foods, not something you are irresistibly drawn to.

It requires time, dedication, support, and constant practice to get past the honeymoon phase because the more you try to stop it, the more it keeps going. By then, you're indirectly trying to deprive your body again. It is possible to go through all the principles of Intuitive Eating until the final one, where you consciously choose to live a life choosing meals that look and taste just as good.

Myth #2: Intuitive eating is nothing more than eating when you feel hungry and stopping when you feel full. Intuitive eating teaches you to honor your hunger and learn to acknowledge your satisfaction cues. However, it is essential to remember those are only two of ten principles. I would urge you to practice them in relation to the other principles.

For instance, adopting the policy of challenging the diet mindset would only serve one purpose: To turn the hunger and satisfaction principles into difficult and almost impossible rules. The obsession with weight and diet means eating perfectly. Practicing Hara Hachi Bu and recognizing your hunger and fullness cues will transform intuitive eating into a diet–one you can sustain for life.

Sometimes, we feel the need to eat in the absence of hunger for the sake of self-care. For instance, if I know that I have a long meeting in an hour, I choose to eat right now or in 30 minutes because I'm not sure when or if I will have access to food. This behavior is part of having a peaceful and respectful relationship with food. Eating when you're not necessarily hungry happens. This is okay.

The principle of acknowledging your fullness can be very tricky at first, because when people are in the early stages of their deprivation recovery, their satisfaction cues are usually on mute and it is possible to overeat. Fortunately, this phase doesn't last long because, after recovering from deprivation, your cues begin to normalize.

Intuitive Eating is not about following specific hard-and-fast meal regulations. Life is not a Navy Seal boot camp, it isn't all beans, bullets, and black oil. Food can be fuel and therapy if you practice listening to your body and mind more attentively.

Myth #3: Intuitive eating is a weight loss program. Intuitive eating is NOT a plan for weight loss. Anyone trying to convince you that IE is a weight loss fad is either very mistaken or is only trying to sell you yet another diet.

Certain people shed a few pounds unintentionally when they begin to practice this relationship with food. Still, some people temporarily regain the weight they lost during their deprivation or dieting period. Few others maintain their weight. According to the experts and research statistics, most binge eaters have been depriving themselves of certain foods one way or another before deciding to practice IE, so in the early stages, there is usually some weight gain. Don't fret. This is normal. Your body is only reacting to the newfound trust and acceptance between you two.

Myth #4: Intuitive eating is impossible or dangerous for people with eating disorders. The principles of rejecting the diet mindset, calling a truce with food, defunding the food police, learning to relish satisfaction in food, and giving your body the respect it deserves are essential aspects on the journey out of **BED**. Research was conducted in 2010 on the link between mental health results, eating disorders, and Intuitive Eating. The study involved 1,500 volunteers who ranged from adolescents to young adults. The study was prospective, which means it lasted for an extended period–in this case, a total of eight years.

Regular surveys were conducted on the participants to gather data on mental health, self-esteem, markers of intuitive eating, among other criteria. The outcome was par for the course. Adolescents who practiced intuitive eating at the start of research and over eight years had minimal odds of experiencing low self-esteem, extreme weight fluctuations, depressive symptoms, critical body dissatisfaction, binge eating, or unhealthy weight obsessive behaviors. These results prove that intuitive eating guarantees improved behavioral and psychological health and are a valuable treatment method for improving mental health and eating disorders.

Myth #5: If you are on a diet due to a health condition, you will be unable to practice intuitive eating because you cannot satisfy all your cravings 100% of the time. It is natural to wonder about people who must be on nutritional plans for health reasons when considering the anti-diet approach of IE. To some degree, adjustments are necessary for people with health issues. Changes are required to help them manage their conditions better. This is done using Medical Nutrition Therapy (MNT).

IE is highly compatible with MNT, as many practitioners have discovered based on years of experience. Following the IE approach in tandem with MNT grants people guidance to gentle and healthy nutrition, which is the tenth principle of IE

For instance, the IE approach will help a diabetic patient explore their general relationship with food and help discover any food restrictions like a restricting-binge cycle with carbohydrates. This approach is highly beneficial, considering the forbidden nature of the food group in their health condition and mainstream culture.

Intuitive eating will also ensure that they honor their hunger to avoid bingeing occurrences. They will also learn to call a truce with carbs and understand that they have unrestricted access to eat, but only while paying attention to their blood sugar levels and listening to their biological cues. IE will help them figure out the right balance of nutrients needed for their body. Intuitive eating is an autonomous approach that works relatively and, as such, an intuitive eating plan for person A might not be the same for person B.

A review of nine research studies in 2015 revealed that individuals living with dietary-controlled ailments also suffer from eating disorders more than generally healthier people. Intuitive eating provides a lasting panacea for these people to handle their health better while creating a better and more peaceful relationship with food.

Myth #6: The less economically privileged population cannot practice intuitive eating. Intuitive eating is not about being entirely in tune with your cravings, but about doing your best to tend to your biological need for food under all circumstances. It doesn't mean consuming the exact foods that will perfectly satisfy every craving. That would just turn IE into one of the diets you are trying to break free from (the eat-exactly-what-you-are-craving-at-every-single-moment menu plan). Besides, that would be too expensive and inaccessible for many people, especially in these times.

Realistically speaking, anybody can practice IE even if they cannot afford all kinds of food. Their plate will only look different from those who are economically privileged. If you struggle with food insecurity, IE will help you figure out ways to honor your hunger as much as you can within your budget. You will discover that you can find consistent ways of having access to food while rejecting the diet mindset and not being judgmental of any body size or food choice by placing them into inferior and superior categories.

Living with food insecurity means you may be unable always to have access to foods that are pleasurable and satisfying and to eat in line with hunger and fullness cues. However, Intuitive Eating wouldn't work if it put this kind of pressure on its participants. It isn't about crossing off every principle. IE is a mindset, a dynamic state of being, and above all else, a practice.

Chapter Eight: Mindfulness

Mindfulness is the act of concentrating on the present with qualities like acceptance, kindness, and curiosity. A life of mindfulness will teach you to exist in the moment and actively savor your experience rather than worrying about yesterday or tomorrow. The past is gone; it doesn't exist anymore—that won't change. There is nothing anybody can do about it other than dwell on it. The future, on the other hand, is mysterious and hasn't arrived yet. The present is here and now, and you have the choice to live it up before you can't.

Mindfulness teaches you how to experience every moment in a way most people don't bother to anymore. It is the most effective way to make the most of the time you have right now. The only time you can smile, think, act, live, create, and make decisions. Mindfulness is a process, one practiced and mastered through regular mediation for as long as you would prefer. This chapter focuses on easing you into mindfulness and the associated practices, after which we will discuss mindfulness as a remedy for binge eating. The link between the two might be a little blurry right now, but I promise you, not for long.

An Understanding of Mindfulness

A practice as old as time itself, mindfulness has been practiced for thousands of years, mostly with religious sects in Eastern cultures, from Buddhism and Hinduism to the practice of yoga. The practice has gained a cult following in western culture due to the high demand for unorthodox ways to relieve stress and ensure wellness. This is seen in the increased number of westerners engaging in age-old practices like yoga and various forms of non-religious meditation. Mindfulness is the English translation of an ancient Pali word sati or its Sanskrit equivalent स्मृति otherwise known as smrti, which signifies awareness, recollection, and attention. What do these words mean concerning mindfulness?

• Awareness: You remain conscious and active in your immediate surroundings. You notice every single detail around you. The practice of awareness is so essential that it forms one of the principal tenets (sutras) of the Buddhist religion, called indriya. This term translates to spiritual faculties, which embrace the strength or abilities of our senses, spiritual, physical, and mental.

• Recollection: You remember all that you are experiencing at the moment and actively store up information long after the experience ceases to exist. A mindful person recalls even the smallest details. "Remember" is the English version of the Latin word rememorari, which means "to be mindful again."

• Attention: This is awareness with a specific focus. It could be a feeling, a person, or an object. With mindfulness, you learn to make better and healthier choices about where, whom, and how to focus your awareness and sustainably.

Let's assume that you intend to practice mindfulness exercises as a means of coping with stress. Maybe you made this choice because you recognize that work leaves you overwhelmed with anxiety, frustration, stress, etc. When presented with a task, your hackles go up like a mother hen about to defend intruders from snatching her young. The moment you realize this, you can redirect your focus to your breathing, tuning out all the noise, and maintaining that awareness until the toxic feelings dissipate. Keeping your attention on your breathing with compassion and gentleness will disperse the feeling in a short while.

The Tenets of Mindfulness

The here and now. This means acknowledging and honoring the reality of truly existing in the present moment. In this situation, you continuously observe the nature of things as they currently exist or happen. The experiences are and should be relative and unique to the observer.

The direction of attention. There wouldn't be mindfulness if we didn't pay attention to the things we choose to pay attention to.

A lack of reactivity. Normally, we respond almost immediately to external stimuli, despite what it is. This auto-pilot kind of response is a product of societal conditioning. At this moment, I need you to imagine and feel like you have a lot of work to do. How did you instinctively react to that? Were you excited, amused, anxious, resigned, doubtful, desperate, or confused? No? Well then, perhaps you felt peeved or frustrated, right?

Do you see it? Mindfulness is less about automatic reactions and more about responding consciously to your life experiences. Mindfulness supports you in embracing your emotions. Once you master this, you gain power over your response. Reactions and responses are two very different concepts. A response is a carefully considered action. A reaction usually does not leave much room for deliberation.

A lack of judgment. Today, it feels almost impossible to remain neutral, sitting on the fence and not picking sides. Mindfulness reveals the freedom that comes with giving up this ingrained tendency to ally oneself with a set viewpoint. You can finally observe situations and people from a detached lens and see things as they truly are, rather than squeezing them through a filter made up of external influence and past experiences.

Being openhearted. Mindfulness concerns the mind as much as the heart. Open heartedness means warmth, kindness, compassion, and friendliness to your experiences while experiencing them. A great example is observing that you think you're pretty useless at meditating. Instead of internalizing the thought and quitting, you calmly and kindly accept that it flew into your head, then let it go and return to your meditation.

Insight into Mindful Meditation

Mindful meditation is a special kind of meditation that has been around for as long as 2,500 years. This meditation does not mean the total absence of thought in your head. Instead, it is the practice of concentrating on a specific object, feeling, sound, movement, or line of thought. With mindful meditation, you can focus on the awareness of the thoughts going through your head, and by paying attention to them, you begin to see specific patterns in your thought process.

The things that go through your mind have a profound effect on your feelings more than you realize. Thus, self-awareness is crucial to handle these feelings. When mindfully meditating, you can choose between one of the following to focus on:

- Your emotions or thoughts
- The rhythm and sound of your breathing
- Any one of your five senses
- Whatever you seem most aware of at the moment.

Mindful meditation is classified into two specific branches:

- Formal mindful meditation. This kind of meditation is always deliberate or intentional. Here, you intentionally carve out some time to be calm and meditate. This meditation allows you to prepare to meditate deeply and better comprehend your feelings and thoughts. It is also great practice for mindfulness that lasts for longer periods with a touch of curiosity and compassion aimed at yourself and your experiences. This form of meditation trains your mind.

- Informal mindful meditation. This form of meditating can happen anywhere and at any time during the day. This form of meditation involves slipping into a meditative state while engaging in your usual activities like eating, cooking, cleaning, drinking, etc. While formal meditation teaches you to be mindful for long periods, this form teaches you to be conscious even while in the meditative state. It keeps you tethered to the present, not swinging back and forth between the past and future. The consistent practice of meditation will teach you to maintain calmness while still being mindfully aware of whatever activity you are engaged in at that moment.

When I encourage consistent meditation, I don't mean rehearsals. I mean engaging in the practice of meditation as often as is possible for you. Don't meditate to achieve perfection. Why? Because it is the wrong way to reap the benefits of this unique exercise. I assure you, there is no need to put your meditation under a microscope. It shouldn't be or seem a particular way because it is your experience.

Mindfulness is a tool that can be especially useful in successfully treating binge eating disorder because their principles run in opposite directions. Meditating mindfully helps you become aware of and focus on the underlying reasons behind your cravings instead of the craving itself.

How Mindfulness Can Help You

You may have experienced the feeling of being lost in thought. Hours feel like minutes as you zone out thinking about something or nothing in particular. Naturally, as you go through your activities for the day, your mind has the freedom to go where it pleases. This is you on autopilot, and while some of these "mindless voyages" might seem inconsequential, the rest are not so harmless. Specific autopilot thoughts and behaviors can be downright habitual, even dangerous. Spacing or zoning out every so often has a scientific term: Dissociation.

Individuals who space out describe their experience as an overload of sensory stimuli or a state that allows their brain to play dead for several seconds. If this habit is peculiar to you, you probably feel like you are in a trance, observing yourself from a non-corporeal standpoint. You don't feel like you're breathing or blinking, yet that is biologically impossible. Your heart, lungs, and the reflex to blink are involuntary actions that cannot be halted by your impulse to disconnect.

Sometimes, we get so lost in action that we miss the little things going on around us, and more often than not, this can mean bad news. Remember all the times you stubbed your toe because you were walking absent-mindedly? Or the times you almost walked into a wall or a glass door? Your legs were moving, no doubt, but you were unavailable and unaware.

With mindfulness, you learn not to stress yourself with destructive and unhelpful thoughts because it will only lead to more toxicity, which usually ends in a bingeing episode. Mindful behavior does not fix the thoughts or problems; instead, it helps you healthily process them, through compassion and a healthy curiosity, while still maintaining your awareness of your immediate environment. This way, it is easier to let go of thoughts that don't serve you. This helps keep the craving to eat your problems away at bay.

Mindful acceptance and resignation are two sides of the same coin. Mindful acceptance acknowledges yourself and your circumstances, the admission of your binge eating disorder and its triggers, and an appreciation of your worth.

Chapter Nine: Using Intuitive Eating and Mindfulness to Stop Binge Eating

Mindfulness, like other skills, can be learned through consistency and practice. This skill does not imply that you gain a mysterious superpower. You merely awaken the self-awareness that was dormant inside you, inside every one of us. Usually, our self-awareness remains dormant until activated by very intense moments, and it is almost always something out of control. However, it is possible to get it out of its slumber and even control it.

Self-awareness is a practice that can serve many aspects of our lives. In this chapter, you will learn how to master mindfulness through brief intermittent moments of steadfast concentration on your life experiences. Let's look at how you can apply this focus to your eating habits.

Try slowing down a little. Americans seem to be famous for eating quickly. I have heard so many people say they just want to eat and get it over with. This American approach to food is not a recent development. Records show that centuries ago, Europeans came into the country and visited the taverns. They were said to be shocked at how quickly Americans gobbled down their food. This attitude towards eating was known as the three Gs: Gobble, Gulp, and Go.

A Tennessee historian spoke about his visit to the colonies in his journal. He noted the rapidity, hustle, and starvation embodied by regulars at the inn. He was dumbstruck at the haste with which the citizens wolfed down their food. Yet another European visited "God's Own Country," and noted his shock at watching many people "inhale" their food like chewing was going out of fashion. Statistics show we are a country with the most stressed and miserable people in the world.

The American attitude to food hasn't even slightly diminished over the years. If anything, it seems worse. Research shows that North Americans spend just 11 minutes at restaurants or the cafeteria at their respective workplaces during their lunch break. The highest amount of time recorded was 18 minutes. Are we all cats on a hot tin roof?

Americans are also well known for maximizing their time while eating. They eat while engaged in other things like walking, texting, driving, and even standing up. This habit seems like a smart thing to do, right? Wrong. So wrong. Americans have an awful habit of treating their food as second place to other activities. An activity as vital as daily nourishment gets kicked from center stage to the sidelines. We tend to eat and do something else like toying with our phones, tablets, talking over the phone, watching television, or reading a paperback novel. It almost looks like the food is a hindrance, one we'd prefer gets handled as quickly as humanly possible.

The food here exists to serve the "eat-as-you-go" mindset. Everything is available to-go, from coffee to Thanksgiving turkey. There is Go-Gurt-Yogurt that can be consumed while driving. The only effort you expend is using one hand to squeeze on the end of the tube while driving with the other. Even adult bibs exist because people eat on the go so often and are prone to spilling food on their clothes.

Asian and European countries seem to think this attitude to food is barbaric and outrageous. I have never been to France, but their attitude towards food is legendary. When the typical French man walks into a restaurant, browsing through the menu is a meticulous process that takes at least thirty minutes. He will use this time to make inquiries with the waiter about "daily house specials" written on the Ardoise (a slate in bistros and diners) or small cards attached to the menu (in larger establishments). He will also inquire about all the possible food combinations before finally settling on a meal. Some French men might even decide on a drink before the main course–the Apéritif –which can range from gin and tonic to pricey, bottled tap water.

I have heard stories of the waiter and restaurant taking offense if a customer glances at the menu and chooses quickly. Even the chef would feel offended if you ate his food with reckless abandon, even worse while engaging in another activity like texting. To the French, every meal is a ritual. The French strongly believe satisfaction is tied not only to the consumption of food but also to the anticipation. The only form of gratitude that the management, wait staff, and chef are interested in is maximum attention to and appreciation of the food and drink. You may not believe it, but to them, this means more than money.

According to the Japanese, eating while performing another activity like walking is terrible food manners. Eating and walking at the same time became only somewhat less outrageous and tolerable in Japan. Even then, this latest privilege isn't granted to much food. It is simply for ice cream cones and only because it will melt if not consumed as soon as possible. Any other meal or drink must be consumed while being comfortably seated.

You must wonder about the fast-food shops littered all over Japan. They are still in business, selling foods like fried chicken, dumplings, buns, and Korokke, the best potato croquettes in the world. There I said it. Take that to the bank. However, none of these are eaten on the go. Instead, they are carried home, laid out on a dish, even garnished, and then mindfully eaten.

Ways to Reduce the Speed at Which You Eat and Drink

Learn to pause while eating. A few helpful tips for practicing pausing mid-meal include:

1. Before tasting the food, pause to take a good look at all the food items before you, noting the plate's shapes, arrangement, colors, and textures.

2. After your observations, be grateful. Spend a little time appreciating the plants and animals that had their lives cut short for you to survive. Be thankful for the people who ensured that you received the food. Give thanks because food is and will always be a gift.

3. Now start eating, pause now and then to savor the aroma of the food. Consider it a part of the nourishment.

4. Have you ever been privileged to see a wine connoisseur at work? That is how you should eat. Breathe in the aroma of the food, take a small bite, and roll it around the insides of your mouth, savoring every taste. If you want to have some fun while at it, try detecting as many ingredients as you know.

5. After that, chew gently and purposely, then swallow. Drink enough water to clean your palate of every food particle, and when that is all, take it from the top.

6. If you catch yourself eating without taking the time to savor the taste of the food, don't chastise yourself, just pause and do what needs to be done.

Learn the art of Fletcherizing. Many years ago, the food blender was named the Fletcherizer, after Horace Fletcher. Horace, sometime in the 20th century, spoke to people about how he properly chewed his food and lost weight, resulting in an ultimately healthier life. His idea, which I think is brilliant, is to take a bite of food and chew it 32 times. If 32 seems a bit much to eat a morsel of food, bring it down to 15 for a start, then progress to 25, then 32, before swallowing.

Pay close attention to the texture changes in the food as you munch. Also, make note of the time you spend eating this way. I advise that you don't get too excited and jump right into it. Begin with eating one meal like this daily. Chew slowly at least once every day.

In time, you'll realize that you practice this for more than one meal daily, and soon enough, you'll unlearn the terrible habit of bingeing mindlessly. Do this exercise with foods eaten during significant states of hunger.

Take deep breaths while you munch slowly before swallowing. Think of every food you send down your throat as a thoughtful gift to your stomach. Try to do this as regularly as you're able to, and watch your eating habits transform from mindless to healthy.

Try drinking slowly. There was a time when I didn't bother to taste anything I drank. I mean, on some level, I knew the drinks tasted nice, but that was as far as my observation went. Are you guilty of this too? When most people drink something, they don't take the time to taste what it is. I mean, what is the whole point of the flavor if not to relish it, really savor it? Do you know what this leads to? Mindless drinking, because we enjoy those fleeting sensations of sweetness.

Taking out the time to appreciate our drinks is a life-changing experience. You feel everything from the explosion of bubbles on your tongue when you take a glass of club soda to the complex fusion of flavors in a Virgin Daiquiri.

There are two effective ways to drink slowly and enjoy the taste of whatever you drink. The first is to keep the liquid inside your mouth for only a few seconds before swishing it around and swallowing. This method ensures that you taste and enjoy the drink.

The second way is to take a sip, put down the cup, and taste the drink in your mouth until the flavor blends in such a way that you can't feel it anymore, then repeat. This method is handy, simple, and reliable, letting you enjoy the taste and drink slowly simultaneously.

You can equally apply this to your food. Scoop some food into your mouth and return the spoon to the bowl. Don't try to even reach for your spoon until you have adequately chewed and swallowed everything in your mouth. To take this to the next level, shut your eyes to help you concentrate on the food you're mindfully chewing. When that portion has been tasted entirely and sent to your tummy, you can then reach for your spoon to repeat the process. Make mental notes of the interesting responses from your mind while you practice this exercise.

Try eating with your non-dominant hand. This exercise is particularly tricky for ambidextrous people because they can make use of both hands effectively. For this exercise, you will practice eating with your less dominant hand, so if your left hand is the one you use most of the time, you will be using your right hand to eat for a few days.

This exercise will feel and look funny during the first few times. Be prepared to cry out in frustration after having to pick up a fallen utensil countless times or catch cheesy linguine pasta. After the awkwardness fades, you will begin to see an improvement in your bingeing after consistent practice. You can't stuff you face at that speed when eating with your weaker hand. Again, it can be very frustrating, but it's either that or regret and shame. Besides, this practice is excellent training for your less dominant arm. This can come in handy if a medical emergency occurs such as an accident or partial stroke.

Use chopsticks. The Asians were up to something genius with this one. Using chopsticks is another exercise to help you slow down and concentrate on every single bite, even if it doesn't start that way. This exercise will work better for people who have not mastered the art of eating with chopsticks yet.

Who knows, it might be one of the best-kept secrets behind the Asian size. Have you ever attempted to binge on ice cream with chopsticks? That idea is ridiculous second only to preferring microwaved ice cream. But for this exercise, it works. For those who use chopsticks effectively, switch to your less dominant hand or drop the sticks after each bite, as you would do with a spoon.

Understand the energy equation. This method of mindful eating is just as effective as the previous exercises. It is called the energy method. Food is a source of energy. Besides our body's need for vitamin D, humans are indirect consumers of sunlight. This ultimate energy source gets converted into other forms before ending up on our plates. Each time we consume anything with some nutritive value, no matter how small, we take in the sun's energy, which we use throughout the day.

If your body weight remains constant for a while, it simply means you expend the same amount of energy that you consume. It is considered an energy balance. However, if you begin to lose weight, it means you lose more energy than you consume, and if you put on some weight, it means that the opposite happened.

We obtain this precious energy every time we eat or drink. We refuel. Sadly, calories will not be absorbed if you sleep, stare at the food, or breathe in the aroma of food as many people believe. You need to place it in your mouth, chew it, and swallow for any absorption to happen. And to expend it, you might need to engage in physical activities. The body burns energy in other ways, too, like thermo-regulation or homeostasis (body temperature maintenance), insensible loss (energy expended through urine, respiration, shivering, etc.), and metabolism (food digestion).

To lose weight, you must choose one of two paths. You can either take in less energy or lose more energy. If you aim to gain weight, there are only two routes. You either take in more energy or lose less. This equation looks obvious, like a stack of numerically arranged playing cards. However, you'd be surprised at the number of people oblivious to this. These options explain the natural body weight fluctuations and hunger level changes. A perfect example is how a good percentage of the population feels hungry during the fall. The hunger is mainly due to the cold weather and the body working overtime, using up more energy to keep the body warm and alive. The body at this time and under these conditions requires more fuel and multiple layers of clothing.

Another instance is during illness. Weight loss happens because your body uses more energy to fix you up than you are consuming due to the loss of appetite that accompanies most illnesses.

One significant way through which binge eaters lose energy is via the binge-purge cycle. Every single time they purge, they lose calories and inch themselves closer to many health complications.

If weight loss is the endgame, the safest and most effective way to do this is to regulate the balance of energy gain and loss mindfully. The little changes matter the most, so:

- Take a walk to shops that are close by, instead of driving to every location.
- Park your car a reasonable distance from where you are headed so you can walk the rest of the way.
- Choose the stairs more often than you currently do.
- Quit candy and soda. Tough but true.
- Leave your comfort foods in the care of any human member of your support system so they can strictly supervise your indulgences.
- Purchase frozen fruits or Greek yogurt as opposed to ice cream.
- Buy your chips in tiny packets so you can still eat them, but in small quantities at a time.
- Consume medium-sized portions initially and then check to see if you need a second plate due to real hunger or phantom hunger.
- Eat the main course first, then give yourself a bit of time to know if you should indulge in dessert or forfeit.

Practice the "out of sight, out of mind" method. Countless binge eaters are prone to the "fits of preference" syndrome. This syndrome means they get a craving, say for cookies, and indulge steadily for weeks–to become disinterested later.

There's a story of a woman who loved chocolate to death. However, a few years prior, she came down with a chocolate allergy. A little cruel, n'est-ce pas? Every time she as much as tasted the tiniest amount of chocolate, she would suffer the worst blisters in her mouth.

As expected, she made several attempts to figure a way around her predicament but found nothing. She tried to abstain for long periods and then try again but in small quantities. It didn't work because even the tiniest chocolate chip would make her break out with blisters in her mouth. She experienced deprivation because this was the only comfort food she had. Fast forward to much later, she came across Reese's chocolate and found it contained absolutely no chocolate at all.

She was overjoyed when her husband surprised her with a large bag of Reese's pieces and placed it in her desk drawer. That's when another problem started. It was only a few pieces at first, indulged in only occasionally, then graduated to handfuls taken daily. Do you know what else became a handful? Her weight. She packed on a whopping seven pounds from bingeing on Reese's anytime she needed a pick-me-up.

She chose not to wallow in her situation but watched her cravings and actions to understand how they worked. She found that the bag right there in her drawer was the problem. Reese's was always staring her in the face, daring her to unwrap them. Each time she felt stressed at work, she would rise to the challenge, dip a hand into the bag, and pull out a piece to unwrap it. She also observed that the proximity between the bag and herself also amplified her desire to binge.

She decided to transfer the bag to her husband's office down the hall. She figured the distance made her less likely to get them whenever she got the urge. Over time, she didn't binge as much, and the thought vanished from her mind altogether. She became mindful of her disorder and corrected it with patience, dedication, and consistency.

Chapter Ten: Support Systems

I'll start simply by explaining what it means to have a BED support system. Your support system mainly consists of a group of people, animals, and even places that hold a sentimental significance in your life. They are there to help you while you are actively on recovery from binge eating. You may not see the need to involve your friends and family because you'd rather keep your BED a secret. There are so many reasons BED sufferers might want to keep their disorder a secret from others. A few are:

- Not recognizing they have an actual problem.
- A deep-seated concern that people will try to stop them.
- Feeling unease over what people might think.
- Thinking you are doing others a favor or sparing their feelings by not telling them.
- Feeling like no one would understand.

These feelings seem perfectly logical from the victim's perspective, so I will not invalidate them. What I would suggest instead is that you let people in. Your family and friends might understand what you are going through more than you give them credit for.

Many observant parents notice when their kid starts hunting for clothes in the baggy aisle, choosing to look like a potato sack in a sweater four sizes larger than their frame. They can tell when you have eaten or when you do your usual table trick, chop your food up into smaller pieces, move it around on your plate, and spill on the tablecloth. They watch you as you continuously dig into your inventory of excuses and lies to justify what they see is going on with your body.

There is a fancy medical term for the denial you face when you suffer from eating disorders. The word is anosognosia. Yeah, it's a mouthful. Mindfully chew on it a little as I explain this deep-seated denial linked to the brain.

You know you have been cutting down on your calories, but you feel you look "absolutely fine" when you look in the mirror. That and you strongly believe everyone is out to get you concerning your continued absence from the dinner table. To you, they are the ones blowing things out of proportion. You probably say something like, "I don't have a problem, you do!" Yet, you visibly cringe and develop goosebumps when served a plate of mac and cheese. The issue with anosognosia is that victims see and believe their version of reality.

This belief makes everyone else powerless to help them, and as such, the denial seeps into the family unit. Meals are prepared with your calorie intake in mind. It becomes the elephant in the room, the topic everyone sees but is scared to broach.

Jessie was 15 and a ninth-grade cheerleader when she first put her hand down her throat. She had eaten two plates of pre-packaged lasagna after a particularly stressful school day. After dinner, Jessie saw a picture of her cheerleading captain in her uniform and imagined the day when she would become a cheerleading superstar.

Then it dawned on her that her dreams may go to waste because of how bloated she felt. Through the internet, she discovered that a serving of pre-packaged lasagna contained 337 calories. That was 189 calories more than a serving of instant ramen! Yet she consumed 754 calories. She rushed to the bathroom, turned on the shower to muffle the sound of her puking her guts, feelings, and shame down the toilet bowl. She wasn't a fan of ramen, but she wished she had it instead for dinner.

To become the perfect cheerleader, she started eating garden salad and an apple every day. She then degenerated to just an apple and mineral water. Thinking nothing was wrong with her new diet plan, she shut her family out, making excuses for her lethargy in school by claiming she had an auto-immune condition.

Jessie confesses that so many days she was exhausted after long hours of sleep. She wished someone would see what she was going through and help her snap out of it.

You might still be in denial as you read this. You don't realize when you're going through a stressful moment or bouts of anxiety and trying hard not to give in to the urge to eat those problems away. There are a thousand ways to care for and support people with binge eating disorder–as a binge eater, you need to let them help you.

Components of a BED Support System

A support system should consist of anyone and anything hand-picked by you. The reason is that you are the best judge of a person's significance to your life. As long as the said person is of value to you, is supportive and more than willing to walk you through this recovery process when you need them to, you shouldn't feel ashamed or afraid to reach out for help. Many binge eaters lean towards friends and family members when building a support system. Others would rather lean on their work colleagues, internet buddies, therapists, and so on.

There are certain times when you might feel so overwhelmed with negative emotions that you'd rather deal with it alone. That's okay. Your support system doesn't have to be a person. It could be a pet or a special place of sentimental significance to you. Try taking a walk to that park you like or any place you feel most comfortable. You can also spend some time playing fun games with your cat or have your dog sit beside you for comfort. Anything to soothe you, for the time being, will work superbly.

How to Build Your Binge Eating Support System

Conversations or quality time with any member of your support system could sometimes be all you need, but there can't be a support system if you don't successfully build one. The trick lies in creating a team dedicated to your recovery, and this isn't as easy as it looks. Thankfully, I have a few helpful tips:

• Draw up a list of your biggest supporters. For this, you will need time to mentally sift through all the people in your life, weighing their significance one by one. Also, put down the names of those who have supported you in the past one way or another. If you think it's necessary, you can also note exactly how and why they supported you. This exercise gives you an inkling of the support you can get from each person. The friend who helped you pick out a dress for a hot date is not the same as the friend who doesn't hang up when you call at 3 AM.

• Draw up a list of places and animals of sentimental significance to you. Even better, if they have helped you deal with your emotions once upon a time. This is different for different people; a walk around Walmart is calming for some and bothersome for others. Sitting on the sand staring at the open ocean at the beach is a miracle for some people. Pick your happy places and jot them down. Take a trip to a pet store or volunteer at the one closest to you if you don't already have a pet.

• A list of all the health-care providers you know is also essential. You will need to start with a BED therapist, then a gastric surgeon, a dietitian, a nutritionist, and so on. The internet is your friend. Browse to see the options available to you, or if there are any specialists you can consult near you.

- Have a conversation with the people on your list. You might want them to be a part of your team, but you need to ask first. They have their schedules too. Make sure that they are comfortable with the prospects of being your support system. You also need to confirm their availability because they can't be your support system if they won't be there when you need them the most. I don't think you'll need to check in with your dog, but you might need to check in with your feline housemate.

- Reach out for help. It is one thing to create a team of supporters, it is another thing to actually ask for their support when you need to. Don't hesitate to seek help.

- Show gratitude to your "support squad" members. Endeavor to be there for them as they will be for you. Make them know how much you appreciate all that they do for you. It need not be anything extravagant, so don't be alarmed. Let them know that they are loved and valued.

How to Meet New People

If you are unable to create a support system because you have a hard time making friends or connecting with people, there is no cause for alarm. I have a few helpful tips to help you become a social larva. Not a butterfly just yet, larva. Baby steps, Padawan.

1. Have patience. You can't form deep and lasting bonds with people in only a few weeks, but it is possible to have regular social experiences with people who you seem comfortable enough around, and who like having you around. It is undoubtedly a great alternative to wasting away at home. Everything else will come in time.

2. Try not to be too picky. Hang out with even people you know are unlikely to be your best friend for two reasons. One, you might have misjudged them initially. Two, they are likely to introduce you to

other friends, and the circle keeps growing. Surprises can be lurking in any corner.

3. Be open to rejection and setbacks. You may realize that you need to send out many invitations before receiving a positive response. Like RSVP's to your sweet sixteen, not everyone can make it. However, be open to negative feedback no matter how disheartening. It is tempting to think nobody likes you, but always remember that there are many valid reasons why a person might not want to or be able to hang out with you. Most of the time, these reasons have NOTHING to do with you.

Remember all those times when you had to turn down an invite because you were tired, in a lousy mood, going somewhere else with someone, busy, had to take your cat to the vet, or even had an interview you needed to prepare for? Many people will be grateful and pleased that they crossed your mind, but they might not be able or willing to walk the mile with you.

If you sign up for evening classes to meet new people while learning something new, you need to understand that certain classes will give you a better opportunity to interact with than others. For example, it'll be easier to have a conversation with a fellow student during pottery classes than math.

4. Social media is a great place to meet like-minded people. It is possible to meet new people in online support groups who also have BED and are working hard to crawl out from underneath that rock. You might even be surprised to meet a few who live a few blocks away. Propose a coffee or milkshake date or suggest you both take a walk together.

Need more suggestions on how and where to meet new people?

    1. Sign up at a sports club.

    2. Consider attending an evening class.

    3. Try book clubs.

4. Join an environmental organization.

5. Join advocacy or peer groups.

6. Engage in activities at your place of worship.

7. Throw a party or attend one.

8. Have your colleagues come over for drinks.

Being a Support System

This job is as delightful as it is complicated. Suppose you are a support system for someone. If so, you are likely to find yourself in awkward positions often because your good intentions can be easily lost in translation, especially when you're offering verbal support. Your comments about things like their food preferences or size and even actions can easily trigger their binge episode.

One of their primary triggers is shame, and it is often unintentionally set off, followed closely by anger, resentment and, lastly, fear. You don't even need to be slightly judgmental or critical to tick them off. This sensitivity is due to their innate feelings of shame about their eating habits and size, so they always look out or expect criticism from others, especially when these topics come up in a conversation.

A seemingly harmless comment like "You have lost a lot of weight" or "You didn't eat so much today, that's great," which started as a complimentary statement might make the binge eater very self-conscious and ashamed. Some are overly sensitive to anyone who tries to control their habits or body size, which seems a little odd considering your job as a part of their support system. They might even give in to compulsive eating as an act of hurt and rebellion.

As a family member or friend who intends to be helpful, begin by having a gentle and cautious conversation with the person. Explain that you simply just want to talk, nothing else. Now express your willingness to help in this stressful time, and ask if there is any particular thing they would like you to do or say to assist them once they start to lose themselves. Feel free to suggest some activities you both can do together, like mindful exercises, as a bid to calm them in the moments when they are overwhelmed by their triggers. You can also suggest a walk in the park or a fun game you are sure they enjoy.

Binge eaters might have similar characteristics, but underneath the urges is an entirely different person. Try to reach out to whoever is under the debris. Sometimes, it is comforting to know that someone genuinely cares with no traces of judgment or spite.

Conclusion

Binge eating disorder is on the rise and is almost seamlessly finding its way into the mainstream media with the young generation as its initial target. Learning ways to handle and convert energy into a productive exercise instead of binge eating is one of the most effective ways to improve your binge cravings.

The road to a life free of BED is through mindful habits and intuitive eating. They are both reasonably effortless and sustainable approaches to eating disorders and life in general. As an avid promoter of simplicity, self-awareness, and better listening, I must state that some level of practice and self-discipline is required to maintain this wonderfully productive lifestyle.

Intuitive eating will help you rediscover the connection between you and your body. Mindfulness will teach you to trust the process and yourself no matter how impossible or difficult it might seem.

I can guarantee you that after a while of consistency and practice, it will not matter how strenuous these exercises seemed at first. You will not actively remember how bored, sad, or lonely you got sometimes, or how often you felt confused because often you will feel deeply in sync with a powerful and primitive aspect of yourself. You will feel an intense level of awareness of your feelings, actions, and thoughts, and that alone gives you an advantage you never had with your recovery from **BED** and progress in life in general.

Awareness of self is beautiful yet mysterious. It is far beyond the comprehension of psychologists and scientists. It is a primal part of us we can only disconnect from but never lose. We are a combination of mind, soul, and body, and so there is no better way to deal with the problem of binge eating than to address it from this holistic viewpoint.

I will wrap up with this: The journey you're about to undertake is not an easy one by any stretch of the imagination. But! You only need to start one day at a time, one meal at a time, one challenge at a time. Soon, it all adds up. And you'll be glad you took that leap.

Bonus: BED Recovery Meal Plan

A meal plan for binge eating disorder helps you get back on your feet, improves your relationship with food, and contains all the nutrients required for your body to function at its utmost best. A registered dietician should design any eating-disorder recovery meal plan. This is because they are the ones with the professional know-how to customize a diet plan in line with your present nutritional state and lifestyle.

This customized eating plan is, therefore, unique for every individual. It considers factors such as weight or body mass index, individual nutritional needs, levels of physical activity, food preferences, and prevailing health conditions.

To prevent the possibility of binges or emotional eating, your recovery meal plan must be structured in such a way that you eat at semi-regular intervals. This way, you satisfy your physical hunger and are not pushed to eat to fill up the void caused by your phantom stomach.

While you may consider restricting your calorie intake or succumbing to chucking certain classes of food groups down the bin, there is scientific evidence that this practice is counterintuitive to your BED recovery plan. Studies have shown that mice fed on a calorie-restricted diet had elevated levels of corticosterone, the stress hormone. This diet led to functional changes in their brain structure long after the mice reverted to their original eating habits. The research also proved that mice with an extended period of restricted calorie intake were prone to eat more due to stress. These findings confirm that calorie restriction in your recovery meal plan could put your entire project for rehabilitation at risk.

The BED recovery plan includes five to six meals each day, comprising three main meals and two to three snacks spaced out over a 2.5 or 3-hour break. Sample menus include different food groups such as proteins, vegetables, dairy or dairy alternatives, carbohydrates, and fresh or frozen fruit. I am nowhere near a qualified dietician, but I have a few samples of BED recovery meal plans, which a colleague turned friend has adopted with a high level of positive feedback.

Her skeletal meal plan looks something like this:

Breakfast: 2 servings of grains + 1 serving fat + 1 serving protein and one dairy or dairy alternative.

Snack: 1 serving fat + 1 serving grains.

Lunch: 3 servings protein + 1 serving of veggies + 2 servings grains and one dairy/dairy alternative.

Snack: 1 serving protein + 1 serving of fresh fruit.

Dinner: 1 serving fat + 2 servings veggies + 2 servings grain + 3 servings of protein.

Final snack of the day: 1 serving dairy, vegetables, or dark chocolate.

My colleague also penned down all her usual binge foods and listed them in order of risk:

Low-risk binge: Mashed potatoes, cookies, fruit, veggies, pizza, salad, fried chicken, or salmon.

Moderate risk binge: French fries, crisps, candy, ice cream, chicken nuggets.

High risk: Burgers, Reese peanut butter cups, chocolate fudge, dinner rolls, lasagna, cake, Cadbury eggs, deep-fried Oreos.

After writing all these down, her final meal plan looked something like this:

BED Meal Plan

Day 1

7 AM

Two slices of Rye bread or toast, a medium-sized banana, one scrambled egg with spinach.

10 AM

Half a cup of cottage cheese with a tablespoon of flaxseeds and a quarter teaspoon cinnamon and a handful of blueberries and a glass of nut milk or dairy.

12:30 PM

Grilled chicken breast and half of a baked russet potato.

3 PM

A quarter cup trail mix or muesli (with dried fruits, nuts, oats, and raisins).

6 PM

Grilled salmon, half a cup of steamed broccoli or cauliflower, one cup pasta, one tablespoon grass-fed butter, and one cup of yogurt.

9 PM

One serving of wheat crackers and two tablespoons almond butter.

Day 2

7 AM

One serving cereal, one medium apple, and one turkey sausage.

9:30 AM

One giant red bell pepper with guacamole.

11 AM

Half a cup of kidney beans or quinoa tossed in a green salad with low-fat dressing, and a cup of soy milk.

2:30 PM

Celery sticks with kale chips, and half a cup of cream cheese.

5 PM

One veggie burger (containing at least 15 grams of protein) on a whole wheat bun, one slice of cheese, half a cup of quartered kiwis and red grapes, and one serving of Greek yogurt.

8:30 PM – 9:00 PM

Dark chocolate with mixed nuts or cucumber slices with half a cup of hummus.

Points to Note for Children in Recovery

Parents should plan the family's meals every week. Make it fun and include the child in the planning and grocery shopping.

You must have at least three breakfast options you can alternate. Buy enough ingredients for your child's snacks.

Remember that meal plans need not be rigid. Make concessions for special occasions and spontaneous events.

Printed in Great Britain
by Amazon